Longman Keys to Language Teaching

Series Editor: Neville Grant

Making the most of your Textbook

Neville Grant

Longman

London   New York

Longman Group UK Limited
Longman House, Burnt Mill, Harlow,
Essex CM20 2JE, England
and Associated Companies throughout the world.

Distributed in the United States of America
by Longman Publishing, New York

First published 1987
Sixth impression 1992

British Library Cataloguing in Publication Data

Grant, Neville J.H.
    Making the most of your textbook. –
    (Longman keys series).
    1. English language – Study and teaching
    – Foreign speakers
    I. Title
428.2′4′07   PE1128.A2

ISBN 0–582–74624–8

Library of Congress Cataloguing in Publication Data

Grant, Neville, 1938 –
    Making the most of your textbook.
    (Longman keys to language teaching)
    Includes index.
    1. English language – Study and teaching –
Foreign speakers.   2. English language – Text-books –
Evaluation.   I. Title.   II. Series.
PE1128.A2G678   1987   428′.007   87–3087

ISBN 0-582-74624-8

Set in 10/12 pt 'Monophoto' Century Schoolbook 227

Produced by Longman Singapore Publishers Pte Ltd
Printed in Singapore

We are grateful to the following for permission to
reproduce copyright illustrative material:

From Cambridge English Course by Michael Swan and
Catherine Walter/Cambridge University Press for page
25; Chuo English Studies Book 1 by M. Ueyama and D.C.
Tamaki/Chuo Tosho 1984 for page 47; New Dimensions
by J. Lonergan and K. Gordon/Macmillan, London and
Basingstoke for page 100; Access to English Book 1 (New
Edition) by Michael Coles and Basil Lord © Oxford
University Press 1974, 1984 for pages 51 and 64,
American Streamline Departures by Bernard Hartley and
Peter Viney © B. Hartley and P. Viney and Oxford
University Press 1983 for pages 23 and 105.

The photographs on pages 68 and 69 have been taken
from Chuo English Studies Book 1.

Contents

Preface

FOR SOME TIME, many teachers have felt the need for a series of handbooks designed for ordinary teachers in ordinary classrooms. So many books these days seem to be written for privileged teachers in privileged environments – teachers with large classrooms, large budgets for expensive equipment, and small classes!

Most of us are not so lucky: most ordinary teachers are short of almost everything except students. They have little time for elaborate theories and time-consuming classroom routines. In particular, they don't have time for long books full of complicated jargon.

Longman Keys to Language Teaching have been written especially for the ordinary teacher. The books offer sound, practical, down-to-earth advice on basic techniques and approaches in the classroom. Most of the suggested activities can be adapted and used for almost any class, by any teacher.

Making the most of your Textbook, had its origins in a BBC *English by Radio* summer school for teachers held at Westfield College in London a few years ago. During an 'Any Questions' session, the panel were asked a question about how one should use a textbook. My answer, which was that the needs of the student are more important than those of the book, seemed at the time to cause some surprise.

Ever since then, it has struck me that far too little attention has been paid to this important question. Yet, for most of us, the textbook is the main weapon in our armoury. This book provides a few suggestions – and, we hope, not only food for thought, but fuel for action.

Neville Grant

Author's note

Many people helped me to write this book. I should like to thank the following in particular: Damien Tunnacliffe, for his patience and publishing expertise; Jeremy Harmer and Hillary Gates, for their very helpful comments on earlier drafts of the manuscript; and of course my students, who taught me so much.

Introduction

Who needs a textbook?

Here are three teachers' opinions about textbooks. Which one do you agree with most?

TEACHER 1: 'I don't use a textbook. I prepare all my own teaching materials. After all, I know my students' needs better than any coursebook writer does.'
TEACHER 2: 'I couldn't teach without a textbook. I use it just like a recipe. Follow it page by page, and you can't go wrong.'
TEACHER 3: 'I find my coursebook very useful. I use it a lot of the time. But not all the time.'

Teacher 1 is probably rather a special case, perhaps teaching English for Special Purposes (ESP). In this type of situation, the purposes for learning English are very specialised. The group of learners is small. Their needs are so specialised that no suitable books are available. For example, it is unlikely that any materials have ever been published to suit the needs of three pre-sessional students of toxicology from Brunei. In such situations, teachers have no alternative: they have to devise their own materials.

However, you may be surprised to hear that there are some teachers of 'general English' in ordinary classes, in ordinary schools, who talk like Teacher 1. They claim to teach totally independently of any textbook. 'I don't need a textbook!' they say. Perhaps you have heard such teachers make this sort of statement. Perhaps you were impressed by them. If so, don't be. These 'general English' teachers who claim to be able to teach without any textbook usually fall into two categories:

1 They have plenty of time to prepare their own materials.
2 They are geniuses. Few of us feel that we can compete with geniuses of any kind!

Of course, every teacher feels the need for some individuality and freedom. We have our own personalities, and we all know that every class is different. Hence the 'same' lesson almost always has to be taught differently to different classes. Even so, it is very difficult for most of us to teach systematically without a textbook.

In addition, most students invariably *want* a textbook. They find that a folder full of classroom handouts fails to satisfy in ways that a textbook can. A folder is no substitute for a textbook. Like a map for a traveller in unknown territory, a textbook is a reassurance for most students. It offers a systematic revision of what they have done, and a guide to what they are going to do.

Teacher 2 is the opposite of Teacher 1: Teacher 2 claims to be wholly reliant on the textbook, and uses it as a cook uses a recipe. Teachers like Teacher 2 argue that textbooks are indispensable. They point out that textbooks can do several very useful jobs:

- They can identify what should be taught/learned, and the order in which it should be taught/learned.
- They can indicate what methods should be used.
- They can provide, neatly, attractively and economically, all or most of the materials needed.
- They can save the teacher an extraordinary amount of time.
- Last but not least, they can act as a very useful learning-aid for the students.

Of course, everybody agrees that the perfect textbook does not exist. Even so, most practising teachers will agree to some extent at least with the five points listed above.

However, not all teachers rely exclusively on a textbook. Many teachers who say that they do, often underestimate their own capacity for *self*-reliance. Many teachers who think they are like Teacher 2 are nearer Teacher 3: they are not as enslaved by their textbooks as they think they are. They may think that they stick closely to the textbook. However, in practice, they often depart from it.

For example, every time a teacher says something in class that is not in the textbook, he or she demonstrates one of the most important qualities a teacher can have: the quality of *judgement*. Teachers use their judgement much more often perhaps than they think they do!

This book is intended for teachers who feel they could do with more guidance on just when, and how, to exercise that quality of judgement. When is it a good time to use a different method from that suggested in the book, to issue a handout, to close the books, or to supplement the book with ideas or materials of our own? For there are definitely times when a teacher should do all these things, however good the textbook in use may be.

The aims of this book are:

- to show teachers like Teacher 1 that using a textbook isn't such a bad idea after all;
- to prove to teachers like Teacher 2 that one needn't be a slave to a textbook: it is in fact easier to use a textbook selectively than it is to use it slavishly;
- to suggest to teachers like Teacher 3 some new ways of deciding when, and how, to get away from the textbook.

In whatever category you place yourself, it is hoped that this book will assist you in deciding how to choose, how to use (and when to lose!) your textbook. This book aims to help you to teach more creatively and flexibly, in order to accommodate the needs of the students. For of course, it is the students, not the teacher or the textbook, who matter most.

Questions and activities

1 Which teacher are you like – 1, 2 or 3? What do you think of teachers who are in the other two categories?
2 Do your students think that they need a textbook? If so, why?
3 'A bad textbook is better than no textbook.' Do you agree?
4 Many people have argued that the teacher is much more important than the textbook: in the hands of a good teacher, even a bad textbook can be made to work well. What do you think?
5 Draw up a list of the advantages, and disadvantages, of using a textbook.

Students, teachers, and textbooks

Textbooks, teachers and learners vary a great deal. In this chapter we shall take a quick overview of the different kinds of teacher, student, and textbook, and the way they might fit in with each other. In later chapters, we shall be looking in some detail at particular textbooks, and the ways they might be adapted in different classroom situations.

Reasons for learning

The most urgent question we can ask ourselves is this: why are our students learning English? A would-be tourist who simply wants to order a cup of coffee, or ask the way to Oxford Street, will obviously have very different priorities from a student who is aiming for examinations such as Cambridge First Certificate or TOEFL. Many, perhaps most, students learn English simply because they are required to do so by their education system. (Gerry Abbott has described this as a TENOR situation – 'Teaching English for No Obvious Reason'!) Some students learn the language for a specific purpose, such as studying. Some may wish to learn English for cultural reasons: for example, they may wish to learn the language in order to study the culture or literature of an English-speaking country. Some may even be learning the language as a means of survival – this might be the aim of some immigrants under certain circumstances, for instance.

Obviously, the reasons why our students are learning English will determine our choice of textbooks and methods. However, our choice of books and methods will also depend not just on the *reasons* why our students are learning English, but the *way* they learn it. This brings us to the subject of learning styles.

Learning styles

Our students are likely to differ quite widely in the *way* they learn – what educationists call their *learning styles*. The way a teacher teaches – and the way a textbook is designed – should take differences in the students' learning styles into account.

Some of these differences are listed below. To what extent can you find these differences among your students?

Some differences in learning styles

A Some learners like to have a written text in front of them. They feel that the written word is a kind of 'prop' or support to them, even when the aims of the lesson or activity are oral.

B Others are happier in the oral/aural mode: they like to listen to, and speak, the language undistracted by the written word.

A Some learners like to be told grammatical rules. Some of these learners – perhaps most of them – would like these rules to be given in L1. ('L1' is short for the learners' first language.) They feel they learn best when they are taught the rules, and then apply them in exercises.

B Others don't like grammatical rules – often because they don't understand them, even when they are explained in the L1. They prefer to 'use their common sense'. By listening to the language, reading it, and trying to use it, they work out the rules for themselves, perhaps subconsciously.

A Some are happiest when the teacher is completely in charge of the lesson. They like nothing better than the activity 'Teacher talks. Students listen.'

B Others like to get busy in pairs or groups. At these times, the teacher acts as a kind of referee or manager.

Can you think of any other ways in which your students differ in their learning styles?

Teaching styles

To what extent should you take into account these differences when you are teaching? This in turn raises the question, not of learning styles, but of *teaching styles*. There are three general views possible. Which of these three teachers do you agree with most?

TEACHER 1: 'My students are there to be organised: I'm the teacher, and I know best. It's my job to decide what the best methods of teaching are. The students just do as they are told.'
TEACHER 2: 'I just follow the textbook's methods. If the syllabus lays down a method, I follow that.'
TEACHER 3: 'I try to find out what suits the students best, and do my best to take this into account while teaching.'

Which teacher do you think you resemble most – 1, 2 or 3? It seems probable that Teacher 3 is the most likely to get the best out of his or her students. But whatever your views, it is clear that the type of textbook you use will have a considerable influence on the way you teach and the way your students learn.

Different kinds of textbook

In this book, we shall use the term *textbook* to apply to both coursebooks, which typically aim to cover all aspects of the language, and supplementary textbooks devoted to particular topics or skill areas. Unless otherwise specified, *textbook* is used to refer to coursebooks. Textbooks are so many, and so varied, that it is very difficult to make accurate generalisations about them. Many of us have our own way of categorising textbooks. For example, one teacher, speaking at a teachers' association meeting in Bologna, said: 'I've heard of *student*-centred materials, and *teacher*-centred materials; but what about *materials*-centred materials?' (She was speaking about some particularly glossy new materials that seemed to have little to do with the lives of either teachers or students!)

In this book we shall try to simplify the discussion by suggesting that there are two very broad categories of textbook. It is not always possible to place a particular textbook firmly within either of these categories, as there is a continuum from one category to another. The two categories are *traditional* textbooks, and *communicative* textbooks. They may be briefly described as follows:

Traditional textbooks

Although we use the word *traditional* here, it is true to say that traditional textbooks are still being published today. So the label is used to describe a type of book, rather than the date when it was published. The traditional textbook tries to get students to learn the language as a system. Once they have learned the system, it is hoped that they are then equipped to use the language for their own purposes in any way they think fit.

Traditional textbooks have all or most of these characteristics:

- They tend to emphasise the forms, or patterns, of language (the grammar) more than the communicative functions of language – the jobs we do using it, for example, asking for information, making requests, apologising, asking the way, etc.
- They tend to focus on reading and writing activities, rather than listening and speaking activities.
- They often make use of a great deal of L1.
- They emphasise the importance of accuracy.
- They tend to focus rather narrowly on a syllabus and examinations.
- They are often attractive to some teachers, because they seem easy to use, and are highly examination-orientated.

There are many traditional textbooks in use all over the world. They have the great advantage that, generally speaking, a teacher can use them without too much difficulty. The main problem with traditional textbooks is this: students work through them, sometimes for years, and often conscientiously. However, despite this, at the end of their studies they are still incapable of using the language: they may 'know' its grammar – *the system* – but they can't *communicate* in it.

Very often, teachers are required for one reason or another to use traditional textbooks. Where this is the case, the teacher has a challenge: both to satisfy the syllabus, and to ensure that students using the textbook learn not just the forms of the language, but how to use them to communicate.

Communicative textbooks

Communicative textbooks try to solve this problem by creating opportunities for the students to use the language in the classroom, as a sort of 'halfway house' before using it in real life. These days, the word *communicative* is on everyone's lips. Almost every new textbook claims to be communicative. What exactly does this mean?

Communicative textbooks vary quite a lot, but very broadly they have the following characteristics:

- They emphasise the communicative functions of language – the jobs people do using the language – not just the forms. We saw some examples of these functions on the last page.
- They try to reflect the students' needs and interests.
- They emphasise skills in using the language, not just the forms of language, and they are therefore activity-based.
- They usually have a good balance among the four language skills, but may emphasise listening and speaking more than a traditional textbook does.
- They tend to be very specific in their definition of aims.
- Both content and methods reflect the authentic language of everyday life.
- They encourage work in groups and pairs, and therefore make heavier demands on teachers' organisational abilities.
- They emphasise fluency, not just accuracy.

What are communicative activities? A communicative activity is any classroom exercise that helps the students to *use* the language they have learned in the classroom in real life. Thus a traditional Latin course, in which students learn how to translate *Caesar transferred the sixth legion to Camulodunum* is not communicative, because neither the skill, nor the language, is likely to help the student to communicate in real life. This may seem an absurd, extreme instance – yet surprisingly often English is taught in a very similar manner.

Some classroom activities that help to develop communicative skills are set out below. The theory is simple: by doing things like these in the classroom, students will be more likely to be able to do them in real life.

Some examples of communicative activities

- Students listen to authentic language for real-life purposes. For example, the students might listen to a recording of an airport announcement.
- Students talk to each other as they might in real life with an English speaker, for example, to find out something they don't know. We call these *information-gap* exercises; the idea is to give the students a purpose for communication. See page 38.
- Students use reading skills such as those needed in finding

information, or the main points, from a newspaper article, etc. which they may need to use in real life.
● Students express themselves in writing in realistic situations, and for realistic purposes, for example, writing a postcard to a pen friend, completing an application form, making notes.

Of course, few teachers believe that all language-learning activities have to be real-life. Some obviously non-communicative class activities have been found to be very useful for language learners. For instance, many students find exercises which require them to imitate the sounds and structure of the language very helpful. Such exercises are drills – they can be useful for learning, but are not in themselves communicative.

Other non-communicative exercises may also be useful: in a modern classroom, you will find communicative activities such as those mentioned above, together with more traditional exercises of one sort or another – dictation, grammatical explanations, and accuracy exercises such as blank-filling and sentence-completion. These exercises have their place too because they suit students' learning styles – or teachers' teaching styles! Often too, such activities may be necessary because of examination styles: many examinations test both the students' ability to carry out various functions in the language, and their knowledge of the language as a system.

A few (not many!) teachers question whether non-communicative exercises are necessary; but it is certain that, alone, they can never teach our students to communicate in the language. Modern courses include realistic activities like those listed above. The theory is that you learn to communicate by communicating. We learn by *doing*.

If you want a quick way of telling how communicative a course really is, try these four communication tests:

1 *Is the language – spoken or written – unnatural?* For example, are the dialogues written in 'textbookese' – or are they realistic? Do all the reading texts seem artificial, or are some of them at least real-life examples of communication in writing?

2 *Are the language exercises all merely textbook activities of a kind no one does in real life?* Or are many of the activities likely to occur in real life?

3 *Do the activities only emphasise accuracy (particularly written accuracy) rather than fluency?* For example, are most of the activities tightly controlled by the teacher, to ensure that the students do not make any mistakes? Or is there enough fluency practice, for example, with students talking to each other in groups or pairs? Note that as soon as we encourage our students to try to communicate – to say what they really want to say – we run the risk of their making mistakes. If some of the activities used in the textbook accept this risk, then they are communicative.

4 *Does the course emphasise study – or practice?* For example, does it spend so much time studying language forms such as verb tenses that it does not give the students enough time to use them?

Apply these four tests to a textbook, and you should get some idea as to how communicative it is. If your answer to any of these questions is 'Yes', you should think about getting a new textbook – or a new approach! But even if you judge your textbook to be traditional, it can still contain communicative elements. And even if these elements are not there, this book will be able to help you to make your textbook more communicative. What matters much more than the type of book you have, is the use that you make of it.

The teacher's role

The teacher's task may thus be summarised as follows:
1 to assess the students' aims, and learning styles, their likes and dislikes, their strengths, and their weaknesses;
2 to decide what methods and materials are most appropriate, given the aims of the syllabus;
3 to decide whether to use, adapt, replace, omit or supplement the methods and materials used in the textbook.

The rest of this book is mainly concerned with steps 2 and 3. Once you have made your decisions in step 2, what should one do with an exercise in the textbook? In step 3 there are five options:

● use the textbook's methods and materials as they stand;
● adapt either the content, or the method, or both;
● replace the content, or method used in the exercise with something you consider more suitable;
● omit the exercise if it is irrelevant or unsuitable;

Listening skills

In the next few chapters, we shall be examining in turn each of the major skill areas: listening, speaking, reading, and writing. However, this does not mean that one can or should treat any of these skills in isolation. Listening skills, for example, can and must be integrated with the other skill areas, so that they are mutually supporting. In this chapter, we shall see what this means.

Until comparatively recently, listening skills have been very largely neglected. However, they are important for two main reasons.

- Without these skills, communication can break down. It is easy to ask questions like, 'Excuse me. Could you tell me the way to the railway station?' It is much more difficult to comprehend the answer, particularly from a native speaker of the language, who is quite likely to produce 'broken English' sentences, full of 'ifs' and 'buts' and 'hums' and 'ers', all pronounced in a non-standard dialect! It is for this reason that modern books try to include 'true-to-life' listening material – English as it is really spoken, rather than mere 'textbookese'.
- Listening is also important because it enables students to learn the language more easily. For example, a student will be able to pronounce a word only after he or she has heard it. Similarly, intonation patterns have to be heard before they can be reproduced.

What are the aims of teaching listening skills?

Listening skills include everything from hearing particular sounds to comprehending complicated messages. Teachers should aim to teach the following major skills to their students:

1 Discriminating between sounds – both in single words (e.g. *pray* and *play*), and in connected speech. For example:
   I think we ought to taste that liquid.
   I think we ought to test that liquid.

2 Recognising (and understanding) various stress and intonation patterns. For instance, the differences in meaning between the following:
   I don't know anything about her.
   I don't know anything about *her*.
   I don't know anything about her?

3 Recognising language signals in talks and lectures which indicate:

   ● when a new idea is being introduced;
   ● when a speaker is going to give an example of something that he or she has been talking about;
   ● when a speaker stops talking about one idea;
   ● when a speaker is making an important point.

4 Overall comprehension skills, which are important in any communication situation. Examples include understanding the main points in a news broadcast, following a complex train of thought in a talk or a lecture, etc.

Using the course listening materials

Most courses give helpful directions for developing listening skills, and teachers won't go far wrong if they follow them. However, there are many occasions when teachers will find it necessary or desirable, to 'adapt, replace, omit or add' while using a textbook exercise. In the next few pages, we shall look at some examples from a number of textbooks.

> The fact that a textbook is quoted in this book does not imply criticism of that book. In fact, the opposite is the case.
> All the textbooks quoted in this book have at least one quality in common: they are all highly flexible. This book contains suggestions for how one might depart from the procedure recommended in the teacher's notes, in certain situations. Such departures are not necessarily better than the author's approach: they may simply be more suitable on occasion. You must be the judge!

Example 1

Discoveries[1] is a three year course for young teenage beginners. The first page of Unit 6 in Book 1 can be seen below. The teachers' notes for the opening dialogue are on the left. In this example, and in all others in this chapter, the textbook writers emphasise that the teacher's notes are not intended to be followed slavishly. If they sometimes seem dictatorial, it is merely because the writers are trying to be as economical as possible in their use of words.

Picture
Ask the students to look at the picture. Ask them to say in their own language where the children are and what they can see. Point to the two attractions, the Flying Octopus and the Dodgem Cars, and ask them to say the words/names after you. In their own language you can ask if they have ever been on anything like the Flying Octopus, and how old they were at the time.

Dialogue
Tell the students to look at the dialogue and follow the words as you play the cassette. Ask them to find the answer to this question: *How old is Lucy?* Check the answer (Lucy is five) and see if the students have guessed correctly the meaning of *too young, only* and *nearly*. Play the tape again, and ask the students to listen and repeat.

LESSON **6** How old are you?

Dialogue

LUCY: I want to go on the Flying Octopus!
ANDY: No, Lucy. You're too young!
JOHN: How old are you, Lucy?
ANDY: She's only five.
JOHN: Are you only five, Lucy?
LUCY: No, I'm not. I'm nearly six!
ANDY: Let's go on the Dodgem Cars. They're OK. Come on, Lucy.

1 Listen and repeat.

11 eleven 12 twelve 13 thirteen
14 fourteen 15 fifteen 16 sixteen
17 seventeen 18 eighteen
19 nineteen 20 twenty

2 Ask and answer the questions.

YOU: What's 2 + 9 (two and nine)?
FRIEND: 11 (eleven).

1. 2 + 5   3. 10 + 3   5. 1 + 19
2. 6 + 8   4. 7 + 12   6. 4 + 11

3 Count like this:

2,4,6 ...
1,3,5 ...
20,19,18 ...

9 (nine)

As it stands, the exercise set out on the previous page will certainly work in most classes. However, this exercise seems to aim largely at exposing the students to the sounds of the language, and to present language items such as *too young*, *only* and *nearly*. These aims are of course valid. However, some teachers would certainly prefer to use this exercise in a more communicative manner first. That is, they would wish to use the exercise to practise listening comprehension. This means asking the students to understand the message, or as much of it as they can, before focussing on its linguistic elements. The lesson might follow these lines:

Possible listening comprehension questions:
A How many people are talking?
B Who are they?
C Does Lucy want to go on the Flying Octopus?
D Do they go on the Flying Octopus?
E Where do they go?

- Introduce the picture, as suggested in the teacher's notes.
- Close books. Play the tape of the dialogue (more than once if necessary). Ask questions such as those listed on the left, if necessary using the L1.
- Open books. Play the tape again, and follow the procedure outlined in the book.

This procedure might not be suitable for all classes. But it has the advantage that from an early stage it teaches the learners that it is possible to understand quite a lot, even if they think they don't know a lot. It teaches them to listen, and to be encouraged by the knowledge that they can still get the gist of a text.

Example 2

American Streamline is a successful course for adult learners. It has a simple but effective methodology, and is amusing and well-illustrated. The approach used in each lesson does however tend to be somewhat repetitive. Typically, at the start of each unit, teachers are asked to get their students to 'focus on the picture' on the first page of the unit. They are then asked to 'mask' the text (that is, hide the words with a piece of paper or card) and listen to the tape. They then listen to the tape again, and repeat the words (with the text still masked). Only after this do they read the words in the book silently, ready for 'question and answer'.

The authors of the course emphasise how important it is to mask the words while listening to the tape. However, students often try to avoid using a mask. The book is open in front of them, and the temptation to break the rules is very difficult to resist.

Book 2 of this course – called *Connections*[2] – is for adult learners just starting their second year (or after about 100 hours of instruction). The opening words of Unit 1 of Book 2 of this course can be seen on the next page. Both the paragraph about the *Sun*

King and the dialogue, are on tape. The teacher's notes are printed on the left. As you see, the students listen to the introductory paragraph first.

Streamline:
Extract from the teacher's notes for 'All Aboard!'

1 Introductory text. Focus attention on the picture. Ensure the text is masked. Set the situation. Play the cassette.
2 Listen and repeat.
3 Silent reading.
4 Question and answer: What is the *Sun King*? Where is it? What is it doing? Are there a lot of tourists on the ship, or are there only a few? Are all of the passengers American? (etc.)
5 Pairwork. Students ask each other the questions in the student's book.

1 All Aboard!

The *Sun King* is a cruise ship. It is sailing around the Caribbean. There are a lot of tourists on the ship. Most of them are from the United States, but some of them are from Canada and South America. It's the seventh day of the cruise, and their ship is sailing from Venezuela to Barbados. All of the passengers and most of the crew are on deck for the captain's party.

A: Hello. My name's Pierre Lafontaine. I'm from Montreal.
B: Hi. I'm Heather Hillman.
A: Where do you come from?
B: I come from Montgomery.
A: Montgomery. Where's that?
B: It's in Alabama. Have you heard of Alabama?
A: Oh, yes, Alabama. It's in the South. I've never been to the South.

Questions

What is the *Sun King*?
What is the *Sun King* doing?
Are all of the passengers American?
Ask, "How many of them . . . ?"
Where are the others from?
Is it the first day of the cruise?
Ask, "Which day?"
Where's the ship?
Where are the passengers?
Why are they there?

The recommended approach could be adapted in several ways:

- Get hold of a picture of a liner or passenger ship – it could be a cutting from a magazine. Display this picture while playing the tape. In this way, the picture helps the class to follow the tape, but the books can remain closed until after the first part of the tape has been listened to. With this procedure, it is much less likely that the students will read the words in the book before they ought to. (Alternatively, if you have an OHP, you could make a transparency of the picture, omitting the words.)
- Ask listening comprehension questions, (i.e. go to step 4 of the teacher's notes).
- Some teachers may prefer to omit, or postpone, step 2, 'Listen and repeat'. It is not clear what the purpose of this exercise is. The first text appears to be intended primarily as a reading text, and is not a dialogue. Reading such a text aloud, even when imitating a tape, seems rather an odd activity at a stage when we don't even know if the students understand it or not!

Comments on examples 1 and 2

In these two examples, we have seen that the initial textbook listening exercises are largely aimed at helping the students to learn the sounds of the language, and to associate these sounds with the printed symbols on the page. These aims are of course entirely valid. However, we have seen that it is possible to use the tapes in a slightly different manner from that envisaged by the textbook writers in order to develop real-life listening skills as well. In our next example, we shall look at materials which adopt a rather different approach.

Example 3

The Cambridge English Course[3] is designed for adult beginners. It contains two kinds of listening exercise – *perception* exercises, which train the students to recognise the sounds of the language, and *interpretation* exercises, which give them practice in making sense of the words they hear. These interpretation exercises aim at teaching the students real-life listening comprehension skills.

In Book 1, Unit 27, Lesson B, there is an example of a *listening for information* exercise. In this exercise the learners listen to a radio sports commentary. The sports commentator is reporting the third day of the Fantasian National Games. As this name suggests, this is a 'pseudo-authentic' text – it is meant to sound as natural as possible, but is in fact specially written and recorded for the course.

On the left you can see an extract from the commentary. (This appears in the teacher's book only.) This material, and much more like it, is delivered at a very brisk speed, just as in real life. It is really quite difficult for some students to follow. For this reason, the teacher's notes suggest that the tape should be played several times. The students have to listen *only* for particular pieces of information – they do *not* have to understand every word. The directions to the students are as follows:

'. . . Over to you, Simon.'

'Thank you, John. Well, it's been a really sensational day here in the National Stadium, with records falling right and left. In the final of the men's 100 metres we had a very fine performance from Arnaldo Higgins, with a time of exactly ten seconds for a national record. You may be interested to know that that corresponds to a speed of just 36 kilometres an hour, so Arnaldo was really travelling . . .'

5 **Listening for information. Copy the table. Listen to today's results from the Fantasian National Games, and note the times and speeds.**

EVENT	TIME	SPEED
Men's 100m Women's marathon Women's 100m swimming (freestyle) Downhill Alpine skiing		

As you can see from the sample commentary on the left, this exercise is likely to be quite demanding. (Only about a quarter of the commentary is reproduced here.) There are many classes where it may need to be simplified. Some teachers may even feel that this exercise is more appropriate for second or even third year learners, and may therefore prefer to omit the exercise altogether. (In fact, the exercise comes at the end of a rather large Book 1, so many classes may not get to it until year two in any case.)

If we decide that this activity is interesting and useful, yet rather difficult for our particular class, how might we simplify it? One way of doing this is by splitting the task up into different stages. The students could listen to the tape several times, focussing on one category of information at a time.

In fact, one curious feature of this particular exercise is that the table omits the most important information of all – who won? There will of course be spelling problems in recording this information, but solving such problems involves good communicative practice. So one way of approaching the task is as follows:

- Amend the table by adding in an extra column for the name of the winner, as below. Write the table on the board for the students to copy it down. (You could also give them the names in advance on the board to make it easier, if you wanted to.)

Event	Winner	Time	Speed
Men's 100m Women's marathon Women's 100m swimming (freestyle) Downhill Alpine skiing			

- Tell the students to listen out for the names of the winners, and write them down on their tables. Play the tape once or twice. The students discuss their answers in pairs, or with the teacher.
- This process is repeated twice more, to enable the students to write down the time, and the speed, of the competitors. Note that in this activity, as in all the others, the right answers are not important in themselves. What is important is the language activities that take place to arrive at the answers.

Supplementing the course listening materials

All the materials we have looked at so far have contained excellent listening activities of one kind or another – even if it has been perhaps necessary, with some classes at least, to adapt, replace, add to or even omit certain methods or materials.

However, often teachers find that their coursebooks do not contain any listening materials, or that the listening materials are inadequate for one reason or another. In such situations, teachers have to *fill the gap* by supplementing the course with suitable exercises, either taken from another book, or constructed by the teacher.

When doing this, it is important to ensure that the listening activities we prepare are efficiently integrated with the other lessons we teach. For example, if the unit we are teaching is about making requests, then the listening material should include some examples of this. Or perhaps the unit is concerned with an area of grammar, such as the use of the present perfect tense with *ever* and *never*. In this case, the exercise should contain instances of this grammatical item. We shall look at examples of integrated listening activities later in this chapter.

Using commercial materials

Commercial tapes should be used when available, because their sound quality cannot be bettered. Schools should certainly build up a resource centre containing a selection of supplementary tapes and books whenever possible. The main problem here is deciding, not just which books to choose, but which parts of the book to use and in what order.

In general, the principle of integration should be followed: choose an exercise in a supplementary book that seems to fit in with and reinforce the other materials in the unit you are teaching. This may mean, for example, that while working on Unit 5 of your main coursebook, you may choose Exercise 27 from the supplementary book.

Making your own tapes

In the absence of commercial tapes, 'homemade' tapes can also be useful. The possibilities here include:

- Taping records and radio broadcasts (where legal), etc. News programmes are a good resource for classroom use.
- Taping various model voices, both monologues and dialogues. It is particularly valuable to have native speakers' voices on tape. However, English is used internationally, so it is also a good idea to tape people who are not native speakers of the language.
- Taping the students' own voices. After the initial shock, learners always find hearing their own voice a useful experience. More advanced learners can be encouraged to make a recording or video as a project – perhaps a documentary on a subject of local interest.

Sample listening exercise 1: with a tape recorder

Here is the kind of exercise that teachers could make up for themselves. All it needs, apart from a tape recorder, is some people to help to make the tape. (Make the recording in a room full of carpets and soft furnishings for the best acoustics.)

The stages in the lesson are summarised in the teacher's notes below. The exercise is designed for intermediate students who are working through a unit in a traditional textbook which focusses on the present perfect tense.

Tapescript

JAMES: John, have you ever been to Portugal?

JOHN: No, I haven't. Have you?

JAMES: No, I haven't. But I've been to Spain. I went there last year, for a holiday.

MARY: You're lucky, James! I'd love to go to either Spain or Portugal. So far I've only managed to visit France with the school!

JOHN: Really? I heard that the school has fixed up a trip to Switzerland next Christmas.

JOHN: A skiing holiday?

JAMES: Yes, that's right.

JOHN: Have you ever skiied before?

JAMES: No, I haven't. Have you?

JOHN: Yes, I went to Austria last year.

Students' answer sheet

(To be copied from the board, or handed out on a worksheet.)

Listen to the tape, and tick the boxes:

Have they ever been to	John	James	Mary
Switzerland?			
Austria?			
France?			
Spain?			
Portugal?			

Teacher's notes

1 Show the class a map of Europe. Get them to pick out some of the countries.

2 Play the tape once. Ask the students: How many speakers did you hear? What were they talking about?

3 Give out worksheets. Tell them what to do. Play the tape again.

4 If necessary, play it again. Discuss answers in pairs.

5 Class discussion.

This is typical of the kind of *teacher-constructed* listening exercise that can be used in class. There are many variations possible, including filling in message forms while listening to phone calls, writing down train times, etc.

'I don't have a tape recorder!'

Many teachers think that listening skills can only be practised if you have a tape recorder, or at least a radio. However, if you don't have easy access to a tape recorder, you can still do a lot of useful listening activities. Here are some of them:

Suggested listening activities

All of these activities are valuable – and none of them need a tape recorder!

- Modelling, for the students to imitate the pronunciation of sounds, words, phrases or sentences. A tape can of course do this, but if you haven't got one, then your voice is the next best thing.

- Issuing classroom instructions, either to carry on the day to day work of the classroom, or to give practice in listening skills. Avoid the temptation of giving such instructions in the L1. Following classroom instructions is valuable listening practice for students.
- Telling stories, anecdotes, etc. of every possible kind. This is an important activity, especially (but not only) when teaching younger pupils. A good source of such stories is the newspaper. Learners enjoy a *true or false* spot, in which you tell a story, and the listeners have to say if it is true or not – and give their reasons if they think it is false. (Today's newspapers are full of true stories that are stranger than fiction!)
- Giving explanations – either about the language, or about problems that have cropped up in the course of a lesson.
- Giving talks or mini-lectures, perhaps on some cultural matter, for the students to listen to, answer questions on, or make notes about.
- Asking questions while focussing on listening skills, and also at other times, too.
- Playing listening games, such as *Simon says*. (The teacher gives a series of instructions such as 'Stand up. Sit down. Touch your left ear', etc. Only those preceded by the words 'Simon says' should be obeyed. Those who make a mistake are 'out'.)
- Giving a dictation.
- Oral preparation for a composition.
- Students listening to each other in a variety of situations – dialogues, mini-talks, simulated telephone conversations, classroom or school drama, etc.
- Attending public lectures, meetings, drama performances, films, etc., that may be taking place in the school or community.
- Interviewing people in the community (where feasible).

As we have seen, the most successful listening exercises are those that are not only interesting in themselves, but which also relate in some way to the other materials in the unit. We shall now look briefly at some examples of listening exercises that the teacher can construct, and give, without using a tape recorder:

Sample listening exercise 2: problem solving

The example below would fit into a unit dealing with sentences with 'If'. The exercise is in five stages – these are summarised in the teacher's notes below. The teacher displays the sketch below on the board, and the students are given this worksheet:

> ## WORKSHEET
>
> 1 Look at the picture. What can you see in it?
> 2 Listen to the problem, and complete these sentences:
>   If the man leaves the goat with the grass, . . .
>   If the man takes the grass and leaves the animals together, . . .
>   The boat will sink if . . .
>   Unless the man solves the problem, he . . .
> 3 What should the man do to solve his problem? (Answer – see page 33)

Teacher's notes

1 Write the title *The Man's Problem* on the board. (If this is the first problem you have done with the class, it may be necessary to translate *problem*.)
2 Discuss the picture.
3 The teacher reads the story. The students complete the *If* clause sentences to show that they understand the problem, and to revise relevant grammatical points.
4 Group discussions. Students use *If* clauses to reject each other's solutions!
5 Class discussion. If necessary, the text is read again. Teacher elicits the solution.

The teacher reads out the following:

This man has got a goat, a load of grass, and a very fierce dog. He wants to take them across the river in his boat. But the boat is very small. He cannot take more than one of them at a time. Otherwise the boat will sink.

His problem is this: he cannot leave the goat alone with the grass, because it will eat it. But he cannot leave the dog alone with the goat, because the dog will kill it. So how can he get them all across the river?

Other ideas

Here are a few ideas for teaching listening skills for those whose textbooks do not contain suitable material. None of these ideas need a tape recorder.

- Listening comprehension exercise: the teacher tells a story, for example, a newspaper article or an anecdote from *Readers' Digest*. The students listen. The teacher asks comprehension questions. Variations: 1 The students ask the questions. This could be a group competition. 2 A cloze exercise: the students are given a summary of the story, with blanks (e.g. omitting all the verbs). They complete the blanks, either individually, or in groups. 3 Role-play: the students improvise a version of the story.
- Using other textbooks, for example, readers, as a source for

listening material. This is particularly effective if the listeners have to fill in a flow-diagram or chart. (See Chapter 5 for an example.)

- Problem-solving exercises. This type of exercise is good because it gives the students an interesting purpose for listening, and encourages them to think while using the language. For example: A man gets into a lift in a skyscraper, and presses the tenth floor button. On reaching the tenth floor, he gets out of the lift, and walks up to the sixteenth floor. Why? Students discuss this in pairs. (The answer is on page 33.)

- Riddles. These may be regarded as mini problem-solving exercises, and again provoke thought. They can be highly motivating. The pupils are delighted to bring in their own riddles, too. Examples: 1 What gets wet when drying? 2 What's the difference between a dark cloud, and a lion with toothache? (The answer is on page 33.)

- Information transfer. The teacher reads out some information, for example, a newspaper report. The pupils are asked to give the gist of the information. Any current magazine or periodical can be a useful source for this kind of activity. Frequently, visuals can be 'doctored' in some way – e.g. by using whitening and students can then label them while or after listening.

- Introducing a reading text or other material. For example, the students have to read a text from a book by a well-known author. The teacher can read out some information about the author and the book, thus practising listening skills, and preparing the students for the reading text. In this way, a listening task can be a very good introduction to reading in the class. (Book covers often provide the information needed for this kind of exercise.)

Questions and activities

1 'Listening skills . . . can and must be integrated with the other skill areas' (page 19). What do you understand by this sentence? Look at examples 1–3 on pages 21–26. In what ways do these skills appear to be integrated with other aspects of the syllabus?
2 What problems can arise when using a tape recorder in the classroom? In what ways might these problems be solved?
3 What level might the listening exercise on page 28 be suitable for? How might you do a similar listening exercise requiring the

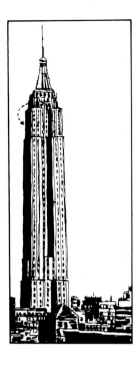

students to state which of the three speakers had ever skiied before?

4 There is a great deal of potential listening material all around us, even if we have not got a tape recorder. Even newspaper advertisements contain potential material. Here is part of an advertisement for *Panasonic* electric shavers where a number of 'close shaves' (i.e. narrow escapes!) are depicted. How might you use this material to give the students an interesting listening exercise? (It might make an interesting problem-solving exercise, for example – see page 31.)

At 6.30 pm on Christmas eve, 1977, Thomas Helms made an unexpected appearance on national TV. An event made all the more unusual by the fact that seconds earlier he had been hurtling towards the New York pavement.

Fortunately for Thomas his suicide attempt was foiled shortly after he'd jumped from the 86th floor of the Empire State Building. Strong cross-winds blew him through the 82nd floor window of NBC News, where he made his impromptu television appearance and regained the will to live.

Something to work on

Listening to a news broadcast can be quite an interesting exercise. The problem is that today's interesting news can turn into something like ancient history in only a few days or weeks. So textbooks are never able to make use of the news in the way that the teacher can.

There are many different possible ways of using a news bulletin to develop listening skills. You could ask the students to listen to the news, and jot down the four main news items. Alternatively, you might ask them to listen to a particular news item and jot down the four main points. If preferred, the questions could be multiple-choice.

Make up, or record, a news bulletin in English, and, working with a colleague, construct a suitable listening exercise for your students.

Answers to the problems in this chapter

Page 30: The man takes the goat across the river. He then returns, and takes the grass. He brings the goat back, and takes the dog over. Finally, he returns, and takes the goat over.
Page 31: *Problem-solving exercises*; the man is a dwarf.
Page 31: *Riddles*; 1 A towel. 2 A dark cloud pours with rain – a lion roars with pain.

References

The examples from textbooks in this chapter have been taken from the following books:

1 *Discoveries* by Brian Abbs and Ingrid Freebairn, p 9 (Longman 1986)
2 *American Streamline – Connections* by Bernard Hartley and Peter Viney, p 1 (Oxford University Press 1983)
3 *Cambridge English Course* by Michael Swan and Catherine Walter, p 111 (Cambridge University Press 1984)

Speechwork

The first point that should be made is this: speechwork does not mean 'teacher-talk'! In many classrooms, it is the teacher who does most of the talking. This may mean that in a forty minute lesson, each student might speak for an average of only a few seconds. No wonder so many students are poor at spoken English! Speechwork, then, means primarily *student-talk*.

In many classrooms, speechwork is neglected almost as much as listening skills. There are many textbooks of a more traditional kind which contain hardly any speechwork. This is very unfortunate, because speechwork is a vital language skill. We all know students who are excellent at answering multiple-choice questions, or blank-filling. But these students may be unable to answer even a simple question in English!

A good textbook will make allowance for three types of speechwork. These divisions are not completely watertight, as one type will gradually merge with another. They are as follows:

- drills, which are aimed at encouraging *accuracy*;
- communication practice exercises, which aim at developing *fluency*. These are graded to enable communication to take place within the language capacity of the students;
- natural language use. It is important to bring ordinary, everyday human speech naturally and spontaneously into the classroom. This is something that some textbooks try to encourage, but really only the teacher can do, for the teacher can interact with the students in a way that the textbook can't.

The rest of this chapter looks in greater detail at these three kinds of speechwork – drills, communication activities, and natural language use.

Drills

Drills are more or less mechanical exercises in which the students practise the sounds or grammar of the language, without having to think much, until (in theory) the language becomes automatic. A drill helps the learner to master some of the basic forms of the language with a reasonable degree of accuracy, before using it to communicate. The most obvious example of a drill is simple repetition.

Example 1: transformation drills

Here is an example of what is sometimes called a *transformation drill*. The teacher asks students to change sentences, like this:

T: I get up at six every morning. Use *Kim*.
S: Kim gets up at six every morning.
T: I have breakfast at seven. Use *she*.
S: She has breakfast at seven. (etc.)

As you see, drills like this are virtually meaningless: they try to practise the *forms* of language – the grammatical patterns – but not their *functions* – the way it is really used. Because of this, in recent years it has become fashionable to attack 'mere drills'. It is true that they are 'not communicative'. However, they can sometimes be very useful, as the two examples below will show.

The drills in your textbook

Many textbooks are deficient in some of the following ways:

- They do not contain any oral drills at all.
- They contain some drilling, but not enough.
- They contain *only* mechanical drills; there is hardly any provision for more meaningful communication activities.

Look at the textbook you use. Can any of these criticisms be justifiably levelled at it? If so, you should consider carefully the suggestions made in this chapter.

Example 2: pronunciation drills

Pronunciation is one area in which any textbook is bound to be unsatisfactory. We have all had the experience of noticing a recurrent pronunciation problem among our students which our textbook does not deal with. So we have to find our own solutions. For example, let us suppose that you notice that your students are having trouble with the /eɪ/ and /e/ sounds. They confuse words like *mate* and *met*, *paper* and *pepper*. These activities may be spread over several different lessons, and should never occupy more than five minutes or so.

1 *Listening practice.* Compare similar sounding words.
  T Pain, pen.
  S Different.
  T Gate, get.
  S Different.
  T Taste, taste.
  S The same.

Later the teacher can write up two lists of words (see left) and ask the students which column the word is in. For example:

pain	pen
fail	fell
taste	test
age	edge
mate	met

  T Test.
  S Column 2.
  T Age.
  T Column 1.

The students should also be given the opportunity to recognise the sounds within sentences, for example:
  T Are these sentences the same or different? Test the liquid quickly. Taste the liquid quickly.
  S Different.

2 *Repetition drill.* Read out the words and get the students to repeat them, first in isolation, and later in sentences.

3 *Production drill.* The students read out sentences, or practise dialogues, in which the sounds appear. If the textbook does not contain a dialogue which can be used for this purpose, then the teacher will have to devise one and write it on the board. This may be the most difficult phase of the lesson, and should be carefully prepared in advance. Here is an example of the kind of dialogue that the teacher might construct:
  A: Would you like a game of tennis?
  B: We can't play in this weather. Look, it's raining!
  A: Oh, so it is. I hadn't noticed. We'd better stay indoors, then.
  B: Never mind. Let's play chess instead.
  A: I hate chess!

Such dialogues should be as realistic as possible and should fit in with the other aims of the unit. In this case, the dialogue would work well if the rest of the unit of learning was about *making suggestions* or sports and pastimes.

While dialogues like this are fine for a few minutes, they soon become boring. So after a few minutes, students can be encouraged to bring in some of their own ideas to make the dialogue more personal and communicative. One way of doing this is by rubbing out parts of the dialogue, and letting them use their own words. For example, line one could become:
A: Would you like a game of . . . ?
(See also the section on half-dialogues, page 39.)

Example 3:
chain drills

Pronunciation of some of the sounds of English is not the only problem our students have, of course. There are many other occasions when the teacher may have to step in and help the students to cope with the material in the textbook.

For example, some students, particularly in the first year or two of learning English, may need help just to string a few words together. Again, some form of drilling may be necessary. If the students find simple repetition too difficult, some modern courses recommend *chaining*, which one can do as and when necessary. There are two possibilities for chaining:

forward chaining. The teacher gets students to imitate him or her, to build up a sentence:
I'd/I'd rather/I'd rather have/I'd rather have an apple.

backward chaining. The same process in reverse:
months/several months/for several months/there for several months/been there for several months/haven't been there for several months/I haven't been there for several months.

Drilling like this may perhaps be necessary at times. But it is certainly never sufficient. This is because most learners find it difficult to transfer what they may (or may not) have learned during the drill to real communication situations.

Communication activities

This is the second type of speechwork that textbooks should include. The theory is simple: students will learn how to communicate by communicating – by *using* the language. Communication activities focus more on fluency than on accuracy.

As we saw in the last section of this chapter, language drilling requires quite a lot of teacher-control. In contrast, in communication activities, the teacher gives the learners more freedom to communicate. They will probably make some mistakes, but that is not important at this stage: at least they will also be gaining competence and confidence in using the language independently. Communication activities often take place in groups or pairs, with the teacher in the background, as a kind of manager or referee.

Many textbooks are deficient in some of the following ways

- They do not contain any genuine communicative activities at all.
- They contain some communicative exercises, but not enough.
- The communicative exercises they contain are not at a suitable level. They are either too easy or, perhaps more commonly, too difficult. If they are too difficult, this may often be because there is insufficient preparation. For example, perhaps more preparatory drilling – or more varied drilling – is necessary.
- The communicative exercises they contain fail because they are not sufficiently related to the students' background or interests.

Have a look at the textbook you are using. Do any of the above criticisms apply to it? If so, you will have to find some solutions. Maybe some of the following ideas will help, but note that they will need to be adapted to suit your own students' needs, level and interests!

Example 4: information-gap activities

This exercise might follow the mechanical drill illustrated on page 35. The teacher gets the students to ask three other people questions like the following, and write down their answers on the grid:

	1	2	3
What time do you get up every morning? What time do you leave home? What time do you arrive here?			

The students work in informal groups. Later they report back to the group, and/or class. For example:

S1: Maria gets up at six every morning, she leaves home at seven, and arrives here at five to eight.
S2: John gets up at five thirty. He leaves . . . (etc.)

This exercise is still highly controlled linguistically, but the words do mean something, and this activity is therefore at least one step along the road from drilling to communication. This kind of exercise is called an *information-gap* activity because students are asked to find out information that they do not know. This gives them a purpose for the exercise – communication practice is not really possible unless there is a real, or imagined, purpose. For this reason, many learners – particularly younger learners – like this kind of activity. It seems to personalise language learning: it involves finding out information, and thus gets them interested and talking about themselves rather than the material in the textbook.

Example 5: half-dialogues

In example 4, the students asked highly programmed questions that used only very limited sentence patterns. *Half-dialogues* are a step up from this: they consist of one half of a conversation, which may involve a number of different patterns. The other half is left blank for the students to complete. They can do this either individually, or in pairs, writing down and comparing their answers and then discussing them with the teacher. Different versions can then be performed orally.

Look at the example on page 40.[1] As you see, this half-dialogue is being used for revision. Look at this exercise, and read the extract from the teacher's notes beside it. In what other ways might the exercise be handled? Can you think of a way that might suit your particular students better?

Example 6: quizzes

This is a good example of an integrated activity, combining reading and writing with speechwork. It is fairly demanding, because the students have to understand the words in front of them before deciding on responses that make sense. Half-dialogues are not used in textbooks as often as they might be. However, they can be made up quite easily to fit in with other activities in the textbook.

Students love quizzes. They can be made into team events, and one attraction of them is that people are so concerned about the information that they forget that they are practising using the language. Another advantage is that the students who are weakest in language may still score well in them. Teachers will have their own ideas about how to organise the class into teams, and what rules to follow. We shall simply illustrate the principle here.

Review

4

You are talking with Fumiko.

YOU: .... ?
FUMIKO: Hi. I'm fine, thanks.
YOU: .... ?
FUMIKO: I'm looking at this skiing magazine.
YOU: .... ?
FUMIKO: Yes, I can.
YOU: .... ?
FUMIKO: Once a year, at least. I usually go on New Year's.
YOU: .... ?
FUMIKO: Uh, not too badly, I guess. But my sister's a fantastic skier.
YOU: .... ?
FUMIKO: She's twenty-five.
YOU: .... ?
FUMIKO: Sayako.

Teacher's notes

Ask the students to copy and complete the revision dialogue. While they are working, write up the unfinished dialogue on the board. Then get individual students to come up to the board to complete the dialogue. Be prepared to accept any reasonable alternative. (The teacher's notes then set out one possible dialogue. How would you complete this dialogue?)

For example, the students have been practising comparatives and superlatives. You could make up a quiz along these lines:
1 Which country is bigger, Mexico or Saudi Arabia?
2 Which mountain is higher, Mount Kilimanjaro or Mount Etna?
(Similar questions could be asked about animals, birds, etc.)

Another quiz could practise the simple past tense:
1 Who won the World Cup in 1986?
   a) Brazil   b) Argentina   c) Italy
2 Who was the first man in space?
   a) Neil Armstrong   b) John Glenn   c) Yuri Gagarin

Of course, the students would be delighted to make up their own questions, which would give them valuable oral practice. The teacher then changes his or her role from quiz-master to referee.

Example 7: problem solving

Here is one more example of an interesting problem-solving activity. This example shows an interesting way of practising prepositions with an intermediate class. Each student receives two handouts – one a plan of a flat, the other with various items of furniture drawn on it to scale. The students cut out the pieces of furniture, and decide in pairs where they can place them. This practises language like:

S1: Let's put the chest of drawers next to the bed.
S2: No, if we do that there won't be room for the wardrobe. (etc.)

Later, different students could explain their solutions. They could use an overhead projector, if there is one available.

Example 8:
guided interviews

Here is a technique that is another step along the communicative road – it provides the students with an agenda with which to discuss their own personal lives. The class is divided into pairs, and each pair conducts an interview on some suitable topic, using interview cards like these below. In this example, the topic is *holidays.*

| A Your last holiday |
| Ask your friend some questions about his or her last holiday. |
| Here are some of the questions you could ask: |
| When did you have your . . . . ? |
| Where did you go? |
| . . . . stay? |
| How long did you spend there? |
| Who . . . . ? |
| . . . . like it? (etc.) |

| B My last holiday |
| Answer your friend's questions about your last holiday. Use the notes below to help you to answer if you wish: |
| Last summer/winter. |
| Greece. |
| Youth Hostel. |
| Two days. |
| I went with . . . |

Later, A can tell the class about his or her friend's holiday. The whole class could then write two short descriptions, of their own holiday, and of their friend's. In this way, speechwork can be integrated with writing skills.

> Would this be a suitable topic, and exercise, for your students? Perhaps you can think of a more relevant topic, or a variation on this idea that is more appropriate for the level of your students.

Example 9:
role-play

In role-play, students are asked to act out incidents or scenes that have perhaps appeared in their textbooks. Most modern textbooks include some role-play, but there are often missed opportunities. Role-play can be scripted, or semi-scripted. Students can act the part, either of themselves in certain circumstances, or of other people that they have perhaps read about in their textbook. Here are two examples:

Role-play 1 The students have been listening to a discussion between two men about two job-applicants they have been interviewing. The students are asked to imagine they are the manager of a clothes shop.[2] They are looking for a new salesperson. In pairs, they are asked to list some of the questions they would ask. Pairs are then asked to role-play interviews. (Here, the students are semi-scripting the dialogue themselves, by preparing the questions.)

Role-play 2 The textbook contains rather a boring reading-for-information passage on Heathrow Airport. The teacher prepares role-cards like the ones below. They are given to different students, who have to improvise suitable conversations.

Student A's card:	Student B's card:
At the airport bus stop.	At the airport bus stop.
You have to go to the airport to catch a plane. It is most important.	You have just missed the bus to the airport.
You are not sure if the bus has gone.	You wonder if it is possible to share a taxi with someone.
There is a stranger at the bus stop.	A stranger starts to talk to you . . .
Perhaps he knows if the bus has gone.	
Start a conversation with him: 'Excuse me . . .'	

Natural language use

We now come to the third kind of classroom speechwork – natural language use. In some countries, there is a feeling that speechwork in the classroom is of doubtful value. In other countries, it may be felt discourteous for students to do 'too much' talking in class. In addition, some learners dislike trying to speak until they feel confident. The trouble is they won't feel confident unless and until they *do* speak!

These are not problems that a textbook alone can solve. It is the teacher's task to establish a friendly yet correct relationship with the class. The best way of doing this is by making natural language use a normal part of the classroom routine. Opportunities are infinite for remarks such as: 'Hello, how are you today?', 'Whose book is this?', 'What did you think of the film last night?', etc. Remarks that crop up naturally can often be made an active part of the students' repertoire: students should be asked to repeat and use the utterance. This kind of language use is so important that its use should depend on classroom opportunities rather than the syllabus or textbook.

In addition to such day to day exchanges, the teacher should also create opportunities for students to say what they want to say, even if the textbook fails to do so. The door must always be kept open for attempts at natural language use. They may not be wholly accurate – but being able to express what you want to say in a foreign language has its own special psychological rewards.[3]

Almost any of the communication activities set out in this chapter can lead to such opportunities. One example here will suffice: in our guided interview about holidays, we should ensure that there is an open-ended question that encourages students who want to talk about a particularly exciting adventure, or incident. In other words, we should do our best to get the students to talk in a personal way about their own experience. This means we must *personalise* our language teaching, so that the learners can talk about themselves and their own interests – not just what is in the textbook. We shall return to this subject of personalisation later in the book.

Summary

1 There are three kinds of speechwork in the classroom: drills, communication activities, and natural language use.
2 Drills are mechanical: they practise the forms of language, and focus on accuracy. They are sometimes necessary, but they are never sufficient.

3 Communication activities give the students practice in using the language under controlled conditions. They are more concerned with the functions of language than the forms, though the latter are still important. These activities try to develop fluency rather than accuracy.

4 Natural language use should be encouraged because communication activities tend to be contrived and controlled. It is important therefore that the teacher should create opportunities for natural language use through ordinary human interaction with, and between, the students.

5 Many textbooks do not practise speechwork sufficiently. Where this is the case, the teacher may have to find ways of making good this deficiency. For example:

a) Drills. These may not be in the textbook, or if they are, may not be sufficient. Sometimes the teacher may have to construct drills to cater for specific problems in the class, for example, pronunciation drills.

b) Communication activities. Sometimes a textbook will contain only drills and there may be no communication activities. In this situation, teachers should find opportunities for using suitable communication activities of their own. Particularly recommended are information-gap tasks, half-dialogues, problem-solving and role-playing activities.

c) Natural language use. It is important to get the students to use the language naturally. For example, opportunities exist in classroom instructions, and incidental day to day conversation. Further opportunities exist when doing reading and writing activities, as we shall see later in this book.

In the next chapter – *Speechwork: case studies* – we shall look at how some of these issues can be tackled when using particular textbooks.

Questions and activities

1 Think of a lesson you recently taught. Estimate roughly how many minutes or seconds each student spoke on average.
2 Now estimate what percentage of the students' talk could be described as:
a) drill   b) communication activity   c) natural language use.

3 What conclusions do you draw from your answers to questions 1 and 2?

4 What are information-gap exercises, and why are they useful?

5 Look at the dialogue at the bottom of page 36. Which words in the dialogue contain the /e/ sound, and which the /eɪ/ sound?

6 The exercises on page 36 are called *minimal pair* exercises. Think of two sounds that your students confuse. Devise similar exercises to help them overcome this pronunciation difficulty. How would you handle these exercises in class?

7 Look at page 40. How good are you at quizzes?
a) Make up ten questions that use comparatives or superlatives.
b) Can you think of another group of quiz questions that could be used to practise a particular grammatical point? (for example, a tense form).

8 Look at your textbook, and see if you can construct a useful half-dialogue connected with its contents like the example on page 40. Remember, your half-dialogue needs to be linked to your textbook in two ways:
a) thematically, for example, if the text is about fishing, the half-dialogue should probably be on a similar subject.
b) linguistically. Your half-dialogue needs to practise something students have learned recently, for example language forms or functions.

9 Here is some practice in doing role-play which you could give to your students.
Look at page 32. Imagine that you work for NBC News. You have to interview the man who suddenly came through the window of your studio at the top of the Empire State Building. What would you ask him? Act out the dialogue with a friend.

References

1 *Coast to Coast Students' Book 1* by Jeremy Harmer and Harold Surguine, p 33 (Longman 1987)

2 See *Framework for Proficiency* by Jane Alemano, p 109 (Hodder and Stoughton 1986)

3 For more suggestions, see *Techniques for Classroom Interaction* by Donn Byrne (Longman 1987)

Speechwork: case studies

In the last chapter, we looked at examples of various techniques for introducing speechwork into the classroom. We also saw that in our eagerness to try out these techniques, we should not forget that the students are human beings who will have their own ideas on what they want to say, and on what subject. This applies particularly to intermediate and advanced students, of course.

Not all the ideas are equally suitable for all classes. Most of them will obviously have to be adapted to suit particular classes in particular situations. This is where teachers have to use their skill and judgement. Let us see how using some of these techniques can help us to change – sometimes quite radically – the approach used in a textbook.

In this chapter we shall look at two 'case studies' – textbooks that are in use today, somewhere in the world. It is of course very difficult to find two textbooks that are typical. However, it is hoped that the books examined in this chapter give us some insight into the commonest problems that we have to face as teachers and the kind of strategies that can be used to reach a solution to these problems.

Case study 1: turning language study into language use

Sometimes, a textbook may emphasise study of the language, rather than practice in using it. In such situations, we have to judge whether the students need to be able to use actively the points of language raised for study. If so, we have to devise our own exercises to suit the needs, interests and abilities of the class.

Here is an example from a textbook in use in Japan.[1] The lesson, called *My Hobby*, begins with a reading passage. This is in the form of a long dialogue between two friends, Yasuo and Hanako, on the subject of hobbies. The three hobbies mentioned are stamp-collecting, playing the guitar, and knitting. The text is illustrated with these two pictures.

The reading text contains rather a large number of vocabulary items, such as *collect, foreign, stamps, guitar, knitting*. Those words that are new to the students are translated in footnotes at the bottom of the page. The reading text also contains a number of examples of the present perfect continuous tense. It is followed by a number of comprehension questions, and this study section:

FOR STUDY

□1□ 現在完了進行形

　現在完了進行形は〔have (*or* has)＋been＋現在分詞〕の形で，現在までの動作の継続，進行をはっきりと表す。

How long *have* you *been waiting* for me?

I *have been waiting* for you for a few hours.

He *has been staying* at this hotel since July 5.

cf. He *has stayed* at this hotel for a week.

□2□ any と some

Later in the unit, there are some exercises in which the students have to write a few sentences using the present perfect continuous tense with *for* and *since*.

Let us apply the diagram on page 17 of this book to this section of the textbook. Turn to the diagram and look at it briefly. As you will probably remember, we have several choices open to us about the content of the textbook, and the method it uses. The first thing to decide is whether we want our students to be able to use the language point raised for study. This question is not as easy as it looks, as we can only decide whether this item – the present perfect continuous tense – is worth practising in the light of other information about the class. It may well be that we may not wish to teach them how to use this tense, because there are many other more important priorities.

Let us decide that the content of this material – the focus on hobbies, and the learning points (grammar and vocabulary) are suitable. (In any case, of course, they may be laid down by the syllabus.) We now have to decide on the method. We may decide that the method is unsuitable because it focusses on study rather than language use. What should we do? The diagram indicates that we have four choices – the four choices listed on the left. Which of these is appropriate? At this point, before reading any further, you might like to consider these four choices, and think about what you would do with the textbook if you were using it. Clearly, we shall have to adapt the approach used. If we don't, we shall have students who have studied some useful items of language, but who have not practised using them enough to have active command over them.

- adapt
- replace
- omit
- add

Adapting the text

As we mentioned earlier, the book includes a reading text before this section. This reading text is in the form of a long dialogue between two friends and contains a number of vocabulary items, as well as examples of the present perfect continuous tense.

Do you think it might be better if the students learned these items by using them meaningfully in speech before reading them in a text? This way, the students would be less dependent on the footnote translations of words in the text. Do you think that this is a good idea? If so, we could try doing an oral lesson before, rather than after, the reading passage. If we did this, it would mean that the students would then be able to read about words and ideas that they had already talked about, rather than the other way round. They would also find the reading passage easier and more meaningful to read. The reading passage would no longer have the job of presenting new vocabulary and grammar to the students. Instead, it would reinforce in another way the language already taught.

Planning an oral lesson based on a study section

Let us say, then, that we have decided to replace the study section of the textbook with an oral English lesson. Two questions arise:

- Given the content of the study section, what should the aims of our lesson be?
- How might we plan this lesson?

Our lesson could fall into six stages:

Outline lesson plan

1 *Revision/introduction*: firstly, the teacher revises any relevant language, both vocabulary and grammatical structures, or language functions. This is also a good time to teach any important new vocabulary needed for the lesson.
2 *Presentation*: the teacher introduces relevant material, for example new language functions or grammatical patterns, in clear contexts.
3 *Drills*: (to encourage accuracy). The teacher gets the students to listen, and repeat, and to do other drills to get them used to the shape and sound of the new language.
4 *Communication practice*: (to encourage fluency). The teacher creates simple situations for the students to use the new language in communication situations. By using the new language to communicate, they are more likely to get it fixed in their minds, and to use it independently.
5 *Explanation*: (optional – to be done as necessary). Not everyone finds an explanation stage necessary. On the other hand, some teachers like to introduce it earlier. It is a question of teaching (and learning) styles.
6 *Written consolidation*: this helps the students to remember the new language.

See the detailed suggested lesson plan on pages 56–59.

This outline plan could act as a model for many such lessons. As you see, the lesson is mainly oral. Clearly the aims of this lesson will have something to do with hobbies – what else can you say about its aims, in terms of:
a) language functions?
b) grammar?
c) vocabulary?

Check your answers with the more detailed lesson plan that you will find on pages 56–59. Note that in our lesson we shall probably try to use the textbook whenever we can. In this case, for example, the reading passage includes two illustrations – one of a boy playing a guitar, and one of a girl collecting stamps. We can use these pictures, and any others (collected from magazines, or drawn by you) to introduce the lesson.

Case study 2: supplementing drills with communication practice

We have just been looking at an example of how one might adapt a textbook that emphasises study rather than language use. No less common in some textbooks, is a different, but related problem: that of emphasising the drill phase of the lesson, and neglecting the all-important final phases of the lesson, in which students use the language to communicate. These phases are necessary if the students are to stand any chance of transferring language that has been drilled under controlled conditions to real, communication situations. Let us see what happens if we include only oral drills in our lesson.

On page 51 there is an extract from *Students' Book 1* of a course called *Access to English*.[2] Look at the extract and answer these questions:

- What is shown in the picture?
- How many drills are there?
- What are the aims of the drills?
- Are all the drills about the picture?
- Would you use this material in your class? Give reasons for your answer.

The picture is the view through a window of a British public library. You will see that the page contains five different oral drills. Drill 1 provides useful practice in spelling and drills 2–5 look as though they are simple question and answer drills consisting of two questions and two answers. In fact, the teacher's notes include a number of other questions and answers for each drill – four or six more questions for each drill, in fact. For example, in the teacher's notes, drill 2 reads as follows:

Short answers with *there is/are*. (Note that the correct responses for drills 2 and 3 depend on the contents of the illustration.)

a) Is there a woman in the library?	Yes, there is.
b) Is there a cat in the library?	No, there isn't.
c) Is there a clock in the library?	Yes, there is.
d) Is there a typewriter in the library?	Yes, there is.
e) Is there a boy in the library?	No, there isn't.
f) Is there a window in the library?	Yes, there is.
g) Is there a map in the library?	No, there isn't.
h) Is there an umbrella in the library?	No, there isn't.

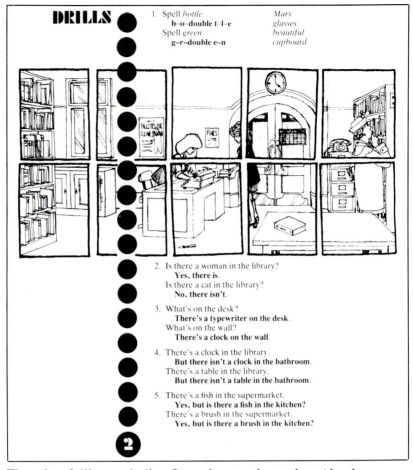

The other drills are similar. In each case, the students' book includes only the first two examples of the drill. The others are in the teacher's notes only. Several questions about this material are worth asking at this point.

- How well do the drills cover the various *there is/are* patterns?
- Are the students likely to find these drills interesting?
- How can the drills be done – with the teacher asking the questions, and the students answering, or with the students asking and answering the questions in groups or pairs? Which method would you prefer, and why?
- Are these drills necessary?
- Are they sufficient?

If you had trouble answering any of these questions, you will find a clue to some possible answers on page 15 of this book – see the four tests of communicative materials on that page. It is clear from the results of these tests that the drills do not use natural language. For example, it hardly makes sense to ask if a library has a window when you are looking through the window as you ask the question! So the drills are only drills – there is nothing realistic about them. The drills are aimed at encouraging accuracy and thus focus on the forms of language, not the functions. One could conclude, therefore, that some drilling like this might be necessary (although these drills probably go on for too long). But it is not likely that our students will learn to use the *there is/are* pattern in any communicative way, because these drills do not show them how. Incidentally, it should be added that placing most of the drill material in the teacher's book has the effect of reducing the students' chances of practising the question forms. The opportunity of activity in pairs is also reduced.

To be fair, we should also add here that the authors do say in the teacher's notes that teachers should use their discretion as to how many drills to use, and how long to spend on them. In addition, they say that the supplementary workbooks give the students practice in communicative activities. However, teachers can't always get hold of such supplementary materials.

Let us assume that we are using a course like this with our students. A unit contains a lot of purely mechanical drills like these, and no communication practice. We haven't got any of the supplementary workbooks. So what should we do?

- adapt
- replace
- omit
- add

Once again, we could consult our list of four choices (see left). In this situation, we could adapt or replace the drills, so that the students could ask similar questions about the classroom, or the view from the window, or even a wall picture of some kind. At least such drills might have more relevance to them than those in the textbook. Alternatively, we could omit the drills – but the pattern being taught is quite useful, and is probably needed in the course subsequently. Also, some drilling of these patterns is likely to be useful.

Whatever we do to make the drills more interesting or relevant need not exclude the fourth and perhaps most important possibility: we could *add* to these drills. What could we add? Well, why not add some communication practice? This problem is one of the commonest that teachers have to face. However good the textbook may be, there are times when the teacher has to make the teaching points in the book more meaningful and relevant to the students. The textbook can never make the materials it contains as personally relevant to the students as the teacher can. In fact, we could call this process of adaptation of the book *personalisation.*

By personalisation we mean making something personally relevant. Personalisation is absolutely necessary if real communication – and therefore useful learning – is to take place. How might we personalise the activities on this page of the textbook? Assuming that we want our students to practise using the *there is/are* pattern, we will have to use our imagination for this. Do you have any ideas about what you might do?

Here is the outline of an idea which you might wish to work on and develop. The precise shape and content of the lesson will depend on the locality and cultural background of the class, so these notes are not a complete lesson – they just indicate what might work. Only you know best whether or not these ideas would work with your class, and how to adapt them. If you feel that they would not work – think of something better!

---

1 Teach/revise relevant vocabulary. Examples: *supermarket, school, church, temple, mosque, public swimming bath, public library, railway station, market, shopping mall, hospital, restaurant, hotel,* etc. (Choose those vocabulary items you think most relevant. Many of these have in fact been introduced in an earlier lesson in *Access to English.*)

2 Drill: ask questions, for example, Is there a railway station in your town/village/street/near your home? (etc.) Yes, there is./No, there isn't.

3 Get the students to ask similar questions.

4 Information-gap activity: students working in groups find out about the amenities of the other students in the group.

5 Class discussion. Students report back, for example, Abdul lives in Qurum. In Qurum there are three mosques. There is a hospital and a hotel. There is a market, but there isn't a supermarket.

Summary

1 In this chapter we have seen some ways in which we could do more speechwork in our class, even when the textbook may not contain sufficient material.

2 We have seen that most textbooks – even the best – may not be right for the precise needs of our class. For example, a teacher may have to help the students to pronounce some of the words, or say some of the sentences that are in the book. In such cases, the teacher often has to introduce drills that are not in the book in order to help the students to cope.

3 In case study 1, we saw that sometimes we may need to present oral language *before* reading, as well as after it. We also saw that studying language is not enough if we want our students to be able to use it: we need to give them drills, followed by communication activities, if there is to be any hope of them actively using the language themselves. This may involve quite a lot of lesson preparation at times.

4 In case study 2, we saw that a diet of drills can distort the language, and make it artificial and unrelated to real life. We also saw that it is not enough to rely on oral drills alone. They need to be supplemented with communication activities, in which the language is personalised. The closer language practice is to the experience of the students, the more likely it is to be learned.

5 We have also seen that the textbook cannot 'talk' to the students in the natural, spontaneous way that the teacher can. The teacher will often have to construct relevant and meaningful communication activities so as to personalise the material in the book – to make it personally relevant and meaningful to the students. This personalisation process is vital if the language is to be used for genuine communication. Among these communication activities are included: quizzes and other information-gap exercises, half-dialogues and role-play, all leading (we hope) to natural language use.

The chapters on reading and writing that follow will show other ways in which natural language use can be brought into the classroom.

Questions and activities

1 Find an example in your textbook of a drill that has no suitable communicative activity following it. Think one up. Remember, the activity must be relevant and meaningful to the students.
2 Look at your textbook and prepare role-cards for a suitable role-play exercise. Make sure that it fits in with the other aims of the unit.
3 Either: a) critically review the sample lesson on pages 56–59. Suggest any changes you would make if you were using it with your students. Or: b) imagine that you are using *Access to English*. Look at the lesson plan on page 53. Can you think of any better ideas for communication practice? How would you treat this with your students?
4 Look at the textbook you use, and do an evaluation of its speechwork component. Consider in particular the allowance that is made in it for: drills; communication activities; and natural language use. Give some examples of the kinds of change you would make in using the book with your students.

Something to think about
- Make a list of all the expressions that you use in class – greetings, instructions, words of encouragement and other incidental language.
- How many of these expressions do you make in English, and how many in L1? How many of these are understood and used by your students?
- Consider how much language your students can learn simply from the day to day expressions used by the teacher. If you are in the habit of using L1 rather than English in your classes, do you think it would be a good idea to use more English – and less L1?

References

1 *Chuo English Studies Book 1* by M Ueyama and D C Tamaki, p 59, 60 (Chuo Tosho 1984)
2 *Access to English Book 1* (New Edition) by Michael Coles and Basil Lord, p 13 (Oxford University Press 1984)

Addendum: a sample lesson plan

The lesson suggested on page 49 of the previous chapter is set out in some detail below. This is a specimen lesson plan and the explanations of certain procedures included here would not, of course, feature in a typical lesson plan, but they are set out here for reference.

This lesson plan is not intended to be a perfect example suitable for all possible classes. It is a plan that will work with one particular kind of class, using one particular textbook, and following one particular course. Many variations are possible. However, the approaches suggested here are included because they can be employed by any teacher, and adapted and used in a wide variety of different situations.

Lesson plan

Aims

Students will:

- learn to ask and answer questions about their hobbies;
- learn the use of the present perfect continuous tense + *for* + *a period of time* to describe how long they have been doing their hobbies;
- learn to speak, read and write the names of common hobbies including: playing the guitar; swimming; knitting; collecting stamps; collecting coins; listening to music; dancing.

Materials

- Pictures and the study note from the textbook.
- Magazine pictures of people engaged in various hobbies.
- Realia: Japanese, British and American stamps. A guitar, knitting needles and wool, a sweater.

Method

Step 1: presentation (1)
The teacher uses the pictures on page 47 and starts as follows:
Look at this picture. What's her name? (Hanako)
How old is she, do you think? (Agree an age – say 12.)
What's she looking at? She's looking at some stamps.
(Teach *stamps* and *foreign*, using real stamps as examples.)
Hanako's got a hobby – she collects stamps. Her hobby is collecting stamps.

(Get the class to repeat as necessary – and deal with any pronunciation problems as they occur.)

Write up this information on the board. Now deal similarly with Yasuo. He's 14, and his hobby is playing the guitar. Use several other pictures in the same way.

Step 2: presentation (2)

Look at Hanako again. She's 12. She started collecting stamps when she was 9. How long has she been collecting stamps? (Three years.) Yes, she has been collecting stamps for three years.

Write *for three years* on the board. Repeat with the other pictures, writing the information on the board as follows:

HOBBIES				
Name	Hanako	Yasuo	Yumi	John
Hobby	Collecting stamps	Playing the guitar	Origami	Karate
Age	12	14	13	15
Started at	9	9	8	9
How long	For 3 years	For 5 years	For 5 years	For 6 years

Step 3: development; drill 1 (third person)

Treat similar visuals in a similar way. Build up this table on the board:

How long has … been …?			
He/she has been	collecting stamps playing the guitar doing karate	for	two years three years four years

(Later you can rub out the second *has*, and write *'s*.) Use this table to ask the students questions. Later, the students should use it to ask and answer questions in pairs, and should use short forms for the answer. For example:

How long has Matsuo been doing karate?
He's been doing karate for four years.
(Short answer: For four years.)

Make sure they include the preposition *for* in the short form – this will reduce the risk, in a subsequent lesson, of their confusing *for* with *since*.

Step 4: drill 2 (first and second person)

Now ask questions like those below around the class. Teach any necessary vocabulary (e.g. ballroom dancing) as it occurs, by mime, or by use of pictures. If necessary, translate.

What's your hobby? (ballroom dancing)
How long have you been doing ballroom dancing? (six years)
Did you hear that, class? (Stanley) has been doing ballroom dancing for six years!

Build up a list of hobbies on the board as necessary. Get students to ask and answer the questions in a chain round the class like this:

A: What's your hobby?
B: Playing football.
A: How long have you been playing football?
B: For three years. What's your hobby?
C: Collecting coins.
B: How long have you been collecting coins?
C: For five years. What's your hobby?
D: (etc.)

Step 5: communication practice; information-gap activity

Get the students to copy the form below from the board, and find out other students' hobbies, and how long they have been doing them. They can do this in groups of four if possible. However, if they are not sitting in fours, and cannot easily adjust their seating arrangements, they can ask the three people sitting nearest to them. A completed form might look like this:

	Sachiko	Keino	Hayashi
1. What's your favourite hobby?	Origami	Gymnastics	Swimming
2. How long have you been doing it ?	5 years	2 years	8 years

While the students are interviewing each other, and writing down the information, the teacher can tour the classroom giving assistance as necessary. Once the students have finished, individuals can report back. Having used the first and second person verb-forms in their interviews, they now have to use the third person to tell the class about the information they have collected. For example:

Sachiko's hobby is origami. She has been doing it for five years.

Step 6: any questions?

Students' question time. In answering any questions, the teacher may refer to the study section on page 60 of the textbook. (The extract reproduced on page 47 of this book.)

Step 7: written consolidation

If there is time, each student writes down the result of the survey in complete sentences, as follows:

Hayashi's favourite hobby is swimming. He has been doing it for eight years. My favourite hobby is collecting postcards. I have been doing it for three years.

Reading at elementary level

Our objectives in teaching reading are to enable the students:

- to develop basic comprehension skills so that they can read and understand texts of a general nature;
- to be able to use reading to increase their general knowledge;
- to be able to decide about their reading purpose, and to adapt their methods of reading according to this;
- to develop the ability to read critically.

Reading is a complex multi-skills process, so it is not really possible to say that only one of these objectives can be focussed on in any one level. For example, it is often supposed that the ability to read critically is an advanced skill – yet every time we ask a child if they like a book or a nursery rhyme, we are encouraging that child to develop critical reading skills!

Since we cannot predict exactly what our students will need to read in the future, they should be given a wide variety of texts in their English course. Materials should include newspaper articles, brochures, advertisements, extracts from short stories or novels, and so on. Textbooks that do not contain a sufficient variety of material will thus need to be supplemented. We shall suggest possible sources of supplementary material later.

We should also remember that texts are not all read for exactly the same reason. Our reading purpose will determine the way we read a text. For example, we may wish to read through a text quickly, to get the gist or main points of it. Or we may wish to look through a text for a particular item of information. A different text may be read for detailed study. These real-life reading skills all require different approaches that need to be practised.

What do we mean by basic comprehension skills?

We referred to basic comprehension skills on the last page. In the beginning stages of reading, most textbooks tend to concentrate on developing these skills. These skills are:

- *Plain sense reading*: the ability to 'read the lines' – to understand the plain sense of what is stated in the text.
- *Deductive reading*: the ability to 'read between the lines' – to draw inferences from what is in the text. This skill involves the ability to draw deductions – to 'put two and two together', and can be done even at beginners' level.
- *Projective reading*: the ability to 'read beyond the lines'. This involves the ability to relate the reading passage to real life – and in particular to the reader's own opinions, knowledge, imagination and experience. This skill should be introduced whenever opportunities arise if we want our learners to use the text actively to throw light on their own experience, and to stimulate them to think. If learners are not trained to read beyond the lines from quite early on, reading texts will always appear as something *separate* from their experience, rather than as *a part* of their experience.

These three skills are brought in, to some extent at least, almost every time we read anything. They are fundamental, and they need to be carefully developed. Normally, textbooks should contain texts and questions that help to focus on these skills. But they do not always do this – and it is therefore important that the teacher knows how to do so when necessary. Let us look at how this might be done.

Example 1

The text on the next page[1] comes from a Kenyan newspaper, the *Daily Nation*. One way of approaching the text with our students might be to ask them to read it silently as quickly as they can, to find out the answers to these two questions:

1 What is a 'turnboy'?
2 What was 'the Naked Truth'?

(Notice that the answer to the first question is not stated in the text, so it is a deductive question!) Perhaps you might like to read the text and find out the answers to these questions before reading further.

Naked truth about turnboy

A young woman from Kakamega discovered it was a man's world when she went job-hunting recently. So she cut her hair short, dressed up in men's clothes and even got herself an identity card under the name of Mr Rajab Maina.

And it worked! She got a job as a turnboy for Notco company and, according to an official, did very well and looked 'exactly like a man'.

But one small slip and all was undone. "Mr Maina" fell off a lorry and was rushed to hospital, where a doctor demanded "he" take off her clothes for a proper examination.

"Mr Maina" at first protested, but had to comply when the doctor threatened to make a report to the Notco boss. So the naked truth was out!

The company investigated the case through the Labour Office and discovered that "Mr Maina" had got an identity card by posing as a man.

Now she is her former self again, Miss Mwajuma Mwania is presenting the company with a problem – whether to lose a good worker by handing her over to the police for giving false information; or whether to strike a blow for woman's lib. and employ the first "turn-girl" in Kenya.

Asked why she conned the firm, Miss Mwania said:

"I couldn't find any other way of getting a job."

(Kenya *Daily Nation*)

Now consider the types of question in the box on the opposite page which are designed to practise different reading skills. You will notice that three question types are listed in the box: true/false questions, multiple-choice questions, and free response questions. It will be seen that true/false questions and multiple-choice questions can only be used for practising plain sense and deductive reading skills. This is because the answers can be objectively right or wrong.

However, projective reading involves the reader in a personal response to the text. Projective questions require students to give their own opinions. It would be absurd to ask, 'It is a man's world. True or false?' because (rightly or wrongly) not everyone agrees on the answer – and some would argue that the statement might be true in some ways, and false in others! So any projective questions have to be free response for students to give their own views. Such questions play an important part in enabling the learners to build bridges between the reading passage and their own lives. If we don't ask such questions from time to time, even in elementary classes, then we are likely to fail to personalise the language in the manner mentioned in the previous chapter.

Question type	Plain sense questions (Reading the lines)	Deductive questions (Reading between the lines)	Projective questions (Reading beyond the lines)
True/ False	The employee's real name was Mwajuma Mwania.	At first, Mwajuma Mwania couldn't get a job.	
Multiple choice	In order to get a job, Mwajuma A married Rajab Maina. B pretended to be a man. C rushed to hospital. D went to the Labour Office.	Mwajuma Mwania couldn't get a job because A she lived in Kakamega. B she was dishonest. C she was a woman. D she refused to go to the Labour Office.	
Free response questions	Why did people think she was a man? What was Notco's problem?	Why did she refuse to get undressed at the hospital? What two dangers faced the girl at the end of the newspaper story?	Could this have happened where you come from? Should men and women be allowed to do exactly the same work?

Reading materials and the textbook: some possible approaches

In most textbooks, reading materials have two main functions:

1 To achieve the four aims listed on page 60.
2 To act as 'shop windows' for language.

This second function means that the textbook displays language items such as vocabulary, structure, idiom, etc. Some of these items may have been taught orally already; others may be met for the first time in the reading passage. The students meet these items of language in the passage, and thus, it is hoped, learn or remember them. This 'shop-window' function is unavoidable in an efficient textbook: just as the number of hours on the timetable are limited, so are the number of pages in a textbook. The textbook writer has to make maximum use of the amount of space (and time) available.

A successful textbook will thus do both these jobs. The trouble is that many texts that do the second job don't do the first very well.

Example 2

Let us look at an example of a reading text 'in action'. We met Arthur – the hero of *Access to English*[2] – in the last chapter. Here he is again. Arthur has driven to a seaside town for the day. He parks his car on a double yellow line, and returns later to find that his vehicle is missing. As you look through this passage, you might like to consider its job as a 'shop-window'. What aspects of the language do the writers wish to display in it?

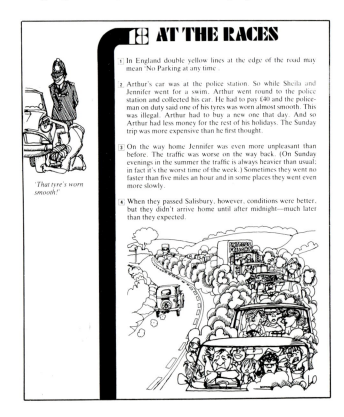

18 AT THE RACES

1. In England double yellow lines at the edge of the road may mean 'No Parking at any time'.

2. Arthur's car was at the police station. So while Sheila and Jennifer went for a swim, Arthur went round to the police station and collected his car. He had to pay £40 and the policeman on duty said one of his tyres was worn almost smooth. This was illegal. Arthur had to buy a new one that day. And so Arthur had less money for the rest of his holidays. The Sunday trip was more expensive than he first thought.

3. On the way home Jennifer was even more unpleasant than before. The traffic was worse on the way back. (On Sunday evenings in the summer the traffic is always heavier than usual; in fact it's the worst time of the week.) Sometimes they went no faster than five miles an hour and in some places they went even more slowly.

4. When they passed Salisbury, however, conditions were better, but they didn't arrive home until after midnight—much later than they expected.

'That tyre's worn smooth!'

This text was obviously written specially for the textbook. The advantages of this kind of text is that the authors can focus the students' attention on particular aspects of the language. You will see that this text very efficiently displays the following 'wares' in its window:

- the simple past tense;
- a lot of useful vocabulary;
- some comparative forms – e.g. *less money, more expensive, worse,* etc.

However, one disadvantage is that reading can become rather boring if it is always written in 'textbookese'. In addition, our students need to have a highly varied diet of texts covering a wide range of human situations if they are to develop their reading skills to the full.

The textbook writers suggest a procedure for dealing with texts like this. Their suggested procedure may be summarised as follows:

Summary of the method recommended in the textbook

Step 1   Pre-teaching of key words.

Step 2   Teacher reads the text aloud, or plays the cassette (twice). The teacher then asks questions on the gist of the passage. (Other options: students listen with books closed; filmstrips; OHP transparencies or wallcharts can be displayed if available.)

Step 3   Read aloud again, stopping after each paragraph, and asking detailed questions on the text.

Step 4   Question and answer work: the questions sound like comprehension questions, but the aim of this work is to practise the target structures and vocabulary.

Step 5   Students read aloud, paragraph by paragraph, after hearing a model reading either from the teacher or the cassette.

Step 6   'Oral reconstruction of the passage' (books closed). Using pictures if available, the teacher helps the students to retell the story.

Step 7   Written work, e.g. dictation.

Step 8   Play the cassette again. Do the printed comprehension questions, or if possible set them for homework.

This procedure is certainly workable. However, it could become very monotonous. It is therefore important that we should develop other approaches too, to make our lessons more lively and interesting. You will find some suggestions listed below.

Alternative approaches – some mini-lesson plans

Plan A	Step 1	Students look at the pictures, either the ancillary wallcharts, etc. mentioned on the previous page, or even just those in the book. Key vocabulary is taught/revised.
	Step 2	The teacher reads the first part of the text aloud (or plays the cassette). The students follow silently, with books open.
	Step 3	Gist-type questions, to ensure they understand the main points.
	Step 4	Detailed questioning, paragraph by paragraph.
	Step 5	Repeat for second half. (New vocabulary is treated incidentally.)
	Step 6	Students answer eight questions in the book orally.
	Step 7	Students now write the answers. (If necessary, this can be a blank-filling or sentence-completion exercise, see page 96.)

Plan B	Step 1	As above.
	Step 2	Search read. The teacher asks, or writes on the board: What happened to Arthur's car, and why? Students read on their own to find out the answers. This gives them a purpose for reading, and makes them more self-reliant by making them do work on their own.
	Step 3	Ask other gist-type questions. Deal with incidental vocabulary.
	Step 4	Treat second part of text in the same way.
	Step 5	Dictation of paragraph 3.

Plan C	Step 1	Revision of key vocabulary, using pictures.
	Step 2	Books closed. Students listen to story once, or twice.
	Step 3	Gist-type questions.
	Step 4	Books open for a search read: the students look for the answers to two or three questions.
	Step 5	More questions.
	Step 6	Half-dialogue/role-play: Arthur at the police station.
	Step 7	Blank-filling exercise of the 'police report', or of Arthur's account of the incident, in a letter to a friend.

Plan D	Step 1	As above.
	Step 2	Books open. The students listen to the text being read aloud.
	Step 3	The teacher asks ten true/false questions on the first half of the text (books open or closed).
	Step 4	Word search: 'Find the opposites of these words': *best*, *sell*, etc.
	Step 5	Teacher's model reading of the second half of the text. Students have two minutes to prepare questions on the whole text.
	Step 6	Team quiz: students ask comprehension questions.

Notes on the mini-plans

- Pre-teaching vocabulary

  Should we pre-teach all new vocabulary before it is met in a reading text? The answer is 'no'. Clearly, if a text contains too many unknown words, then our students will become frustrated. But if we always pre-teach new vocabulary, then the students will not have the opportunity of developing the skill of *word-inference* – working out the meaning of a word from the way it is used.

- Pre-reading questions

  Should we ask pre-reading questions, as in mini-plan B? It is a good idea to do so, because this gives the students a purpose for reading, and makes it a more meaningful and interesting activity.

- Oral questioning

  Should we always ask questions orally, rather than getting the students to write the answers to those given in the book? The answer is 'at this level, yes'. The textbook's questions are very seldom exactly suitable for our students. Often they test, rather than train. Often they are insufficient – important questions are omitted. Often they are too hard, or too easy. While asking oral questions, we can swiftly tell whether the students are having comprehension difficulties. If necessary, we can rephrase the question, to help clarify the meaning, in a way the book can't.

- Reading aloud

  There is no point in getting students to read a text aloud unless and until they have understood it. Even after they have done so, there is not a lot of point in their reading aloud except as an exercise in voice-production. But as prose read aloud is not the same as spoken language, reading aloud is best kept for dialogues, and the occasional poem. It should be noted that reading aloud does not play an important part in developing reading skills and if it is overdone, it can slow students' reading speeds down. We can read silently much more quickly than we can read aloud.

● Other activities

Many activities in a reading lesson are not directly connected with reading skills, for example, oral question and answer is as much a way of practising speechwork as of practising comprehension. The more we can get our students to read and talk, and to talk and read, (and to write a bit as well) the better they will perform in all their language skills. One skill can reinforce the others. For this reason, follow-up activities such as half-dialogues, role-play, dictation, etc. are very important.

Example 3

Let us now look at a different kind of text from a different textbook.[3] This textbook has a much wider variety of texts in it, including dialogues like the one in the example below.

Lesson 8

Shakespeare's Plays

Cindy : How often a month do you usually go to the theater ?

Karen : Once or twice. I went to the theater last Saturday and saw *King Lear.*

Cindy : Did you read Shakespeare's four great ⁵ tragedies ? They are *Hamlet, Othello, Macbeth* and *King Lear.*

Karen : Yes, I not only read them but also saw them on the stage.

Cindy : Which do you like better, *Macbeth* or *Othello?* ₁₀

Karen : I like *Macbeth* better than *Othello.*

Cindy : Which do you like best of them all ?

Shakespeare [ʃéikspiər] 「シェイクスピア」 **play** [plei] 図「劇」 **2. theater** [θíːətər/θíətə] 「劇場」 **3. twice** [twais] 「二度」 **4. Lear** [liər] 「リア」 **6. tragedy** [trǽdʒidi] 「悲劇」 **6. Hamlet** [hǽmlit] 「ハムレット」 **6. Othello** [o{u}θélou] 「オセロ」 **6. Macbeth** [məkbéθ] 「マクベス」 **8. not only A but also B** 「AだけでなくBも」 **9. stage** [steidʒ] 「舞台」

— 33 —

> **⑧ SHAKESPEARE'S PLAYS**
>
> *Karen :* I like *Hamlet* best.
>
> *Cindy :* Was Hamlet prince of England?
>
> *Karen :* No, he was prince of Denmark.
>
> *Cindy :* Did he become king of Denmark?
>
> 5 *Karen :* No, he didn't. His friend killed him by mistake.
>
>
>
> *Hamlet*, Act III, Scene 1 (Hamlet and Ophelia)
>
> ══ **QUESTIONS** ══
>
> 〔A〕 本文の内容と一致するものを選びなさい。
>
> 1. Karen goes to the theater once or twice a month.
> 2. Karen didn't read *Hamlet* but saw it on the stage.
> 3. Karen likes *Macbeth* better than *Othello*.
> 4. Hamlet was prince of England.
> 5. Hamlet killed his friend by mistake.
>
> 2. **prince** [prins] 「王子」   3. **Denmark** [dénmɑːrk] 「デンマーク」
> 5. **by mistake** [mistéik] 「間違って」
>
> — 34 —

Note: This text uses the conventions of American English – as you will see from the spelling of theatre – *theater* in American English. More significant is the use of the simple past tense for the question, 'Did you read Shakespeare's four great tragedies?' In standard British English, the present perfect would be used: 'Have you read Shakespeare's four great tragedies?'

Discussion

● As we saw in the last chapter, this book begins each lesson with a reading text. Points illustrated in the text are then selected for study, and exercises. Can you guess what language points are identified here for further study?

● We also saw in the last chapter that it may be best when handling this book to reverse the order in which the material is treated. In other words, we should teach an oral lesson, focussing on the study points identified in the book, before reading. In this case, the study points are the present simple tense for talking about habitual events, (together with adverbs such as *always, sometimes, usually* and *never*), and the comparatives and superlatives of *good, well, much, many, little,* and *bad.* These features of the language, then, should be pre-taught in what *Access to English* calls 'Preliminary Teaching Points'. We saw one way of doing this in the sample lesson at the end of Chapter 3.

● Let us assume that the students have been given plenty of practice in using these items, talking about their own lives and interests, so that the language is student-centred rather than 'text-centred'. How should we approach this reading passage? On the next page we suggest some answers.

Translation

Just before we look at possible ways of treating this text, it might be as well to mention briefly the question of translation. Often a word can conveniently be taught by translation. For example, the word *legal* that appeared in the last text we looked at, could probably best be handled by a quick translation, rather than a time-wasting explanation. Time adverbs like *always* may also be good items to translate. But just as often, translation is unnecessary. Psychologically, the ideal is for the English word to be directly associated with the concept it represents.

Thus in the text there are the words *play, theatre, stage,* and *tragedy.* Which of these might be better treated by reference to a picture of some kind, and which might be most quickly and conveniently taught by translation?

A possible approach

Many of the approaches and activities mentioned on pages 65–67 of this chapter are also relevant here. One possible mini-plan, following a fairly traditional pattern, might be as follows:

Step 1   Introduction
Show a picture of Shakespeare. Talk about him in English. Find out what the students know about him. Make sure they know roughly who he is, and the fact that he wrote plays. (Teach *play, tragedy,* and *theatre* by translation.) Make sure that you do not give away any information that might sabotage the listening comprehension exercise you have planned.

Step 2 Listening comprehension
A good, functional, communicative exercise (see Chapter 2). The teacher will have to make up a suitable text, and questions. (The text should of course be about William Shakespeare . . .)

Step 3 Tell them you are going to play a recording of Cindy's conversation with Karen. Play a cassette of the dialogue. Books shut. (If possible get native English speakers to make the recording.) Ask gist-type questions such as:
How many speakers could you hear?
How often does Karen go to the theatre?
When did Karen see the play King Lear? (etc.)

Step 4 Books open. Play the cassette again, in sections. Ask the same questions, and supplementaries, as necessary, dealing with any vocabulary or pronunciation problems as they occur.

Step 5 Do the true/false questions in section A orally.

Step 6 Play the cassette again, line by line. Get the students to repeat and/or *shadow* the speaker. (Shadowing means that they read it aloud softly at the same time as the speaker on the cassette.) They can do this first chorally, and then individually. If the class is very large, get one half to read Cindy's words, and one half Karen's, then change over.

Step 7 Students read through the dialogue in pairs.

Look at this mini-plan, and the suggested variations below. If you were handling this text with your class, which of the steps would you choose to work through, and which would you omit?

Variations

- 'Jigsaw reading' (steps 3, 4 or 5)
  Books closed. The students are given the dialogue, cut up into speech units. In pairs, they arrange it in the correct order.
- Memorisation in pairs (steps 4, 5 or 6)
  Allocate small chunks of dialogue – not more than four speeches – to different pairs. Get them to rehearse and memorise them, ready for a performance in front of the class. This can be done with a good class, with whom the teacher has a warm relationship.
- Class memorisation
  Write up an exchange (of about four speeches or so) on the board.

Get students to read it out. Gradually delete words and phrases, until the whole dialogue is rubbed out – and the class have memorised the speech.

- Parallel dialogues
  Working in pairs, the students make up their own dialogues so they are true for them. Thus the dialogue might start:
  S1: How often do you usually go to the cinema? (etc.)

- Role-play
  After preparing parallel dialogues, the students can perform them in front of the class.

- Summary writing
  The students could complete this summary:
  Karen _____ to the theatre once or twice a month. Last Saturday she _____ King Lear. She _____ she has read all of Shakespeare's tragedies. The play she _____ most is Hamlet.

- Dictation
  Alternatively, the complete summary could be dictated.

More authentic approaches

The approaches we have been looking at so far in examples 1 and 2 have emphasised three things:
1 The use of artificial language-learning texts.
2 Detailed understanding of the text almost word by word.
3 The use of the text as a basis for controlled oral work of one sort or another. (Sometimes the questions the teacher asks are designed to practise particular structures.)

There are many situations where this kind of approach may be necessary. It is true that the texts created in this way often seem stilted and unnatural. However, even if we may sometimes dislike the reading texts in a book for this reason, it is not easy to omit them. At elementary level, the text plays an important role in the language-learning process. It is closely integrated with other elements in the course, such as grammar and vocabulary development, and cannot easily be omitted or replaced. In addition, many learners find that this kind of text-based oral work does seem to help them to learn the language.

The problem is this: many pupils who learned to 'read' through this method never develop their reading skills in English. This is because approaches like these tend to teach bad habits like:

- reading aloud (rather than reading silently, which is how most of us have to learn to read in real life);
- reading word by word – the questions tend to focus attention on every word in the text. Research indicates that efficient readers do not read in this way: they read words in units of meaning (phrases) and skip them if they are not essential;
- reading slowly. The approach tends to result in students reading very slowly;
- relying on the teacher too much. It is vital that students rely on their own reading skills to get the meaning from the text.

So if you have texts like these in your textbook, and you find lessons like these a useful way of learning or practising language, you are urged very strongly to employ an additional approach to reading in your classroom. We may call this the *authentic* approach or the *real-life* approach.

The authentic approach means the following:

- The text is (or appears to be) authentic – in other words it is a text that could appear outside the classroom in real life.
- The tasks we ask the learners to perform are realistic, and thus help to develop real-life reading skills.

The approach is summarised by Jeremy Harmer in his teacher's notes to his course *Meridian*:

'The main thing to remember is that the students should read the texts without worrying about the meaning of every individual word. The idea is for them to get a general idea of the meaning of the text and to acquire confidence gradually when faced with written English.'

Example 4

Here is an example.[4] The exercise is for beginners – yet already, the book is developing in the students the idea that they can get the meaning from the text independently, without the teacher acting as a sort of midwife! Another interesting feature of the exercise is that it encourages oral interaction between the students. The teacher is not a 'question master', but is simply an organiser. Study the teacher's notes on page 74 first of all.

In this lesson . . .

Students are exposed to a reading passage for the first time and are asked to treat it in a special way. It is important to be clear about the procedures you wish the students to follow since this first exposure could determine the students' reaction to reading in this course.

Teaching stages

- Get students to look at the text, but not read it. Ask them to say anything they can about it. Do not worry about the accuracy of what they are saying, but encourage them to try and get over facts such as that the advertisement has got something to do with aeroplanes, etc.

Reading

1

- Tell students to read questions 1–3 in exercise 1. They should not read the text at this stage.
- Go through the questions with the students making sure that they understand them. You will need to explain the meaning of the words *advertisement* and *happy*, and the verb phrase *does he travel*.
- Tell students to read the text as quickly as possible and to answer the questions. When they have done this they can compare their findings with a neighbour.
- Go through the answers with the students: 1 Yes, it is an advertisement (for ACE airlines). 2 Yes, Christopher Williams is happy in his job. (He is smiling in the picture. He says 'I like being a steward.') 3 Yes, he does travel to North America and Canada. ('Now I travel to North America, Canada and Africa.')

2

- Tell students to look at exercise 2. Put them in pairs or small groups to complete the task. You can go round checking their answers if the class is fairly small. Otherwise you can draw the diagram on the board and have students come up and complete it with (clockwise from top right) Europe, Africa, South America, North America.
- Tell the students that they can ask you for the meaning of words in the text. (You should limit the number of words for reasons of time.) If students have dictionaries they can look up such words rather than ask the teacher. You should be prepared to help the students with any difficulties that they have during this stage.

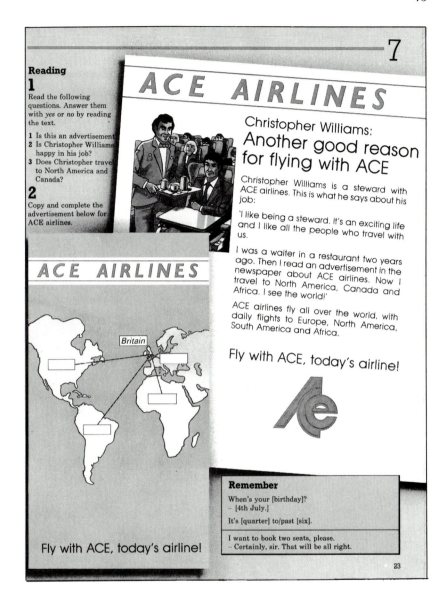

ACE AIRLINES

Reading

1

Read the following questions. Answer them with *yes* or *no* by reading the text.

1 Is this an advertisement?
2 Is Christopher Williams happy in his job?
3 Does Christopher travel to North America and Canada?

2

Copy and complete the advertisement below for ACE airlines.

7

Christopher Williams:
Another good reason for flying with ACE

Christopher Williams is a steward with ACE airlines. This is what he says about his job:

'I like being a steward. It's an exciting life and I like all the people who travel with us.

I was a waiter in a restaurant two years ago. Then I read an advertisement in the newspaper about ACE airlines. Now I travel to North America, Canada and Africa. I see the world!'

ACE airlines fly all over the world, with daily flights to Europe, North America, South America and Africa.

Fly with ACE, today's airline!

Britain

ACE AIRLINES

Fly with ACE, today's airline!

Remember

When's your [birthday]?
– [4th July.]

It's [quarter] to/past [six].

I want to book two seats, please.
– Certainly, sir. That will be all right.

23

Summary

1 In this chapter we focussed mainly on the early stages of reading, when the main priorities are developing basic reading comprehension skills and language development.

2 Many textbooks lack sufficient guidance on how to introduce a reading text, to help students 'attack' it. Possible ways of doing this include any combination of the following: a listening exercise; using visuals; and pre-teaching crucial vocabulary. Asking pre-reading questions, particularly with authentic or pseudo-authentic texts make the reading exercise more interesting and purposeful.

3 The teacher's oral questioning can act as an important bridge between the students and the written text. Some textbooks suggest this kind of oral work, usually in the teacher's notes. However, oral discussion is essential even when the textbook does not suggest it. Oral discussions do not have to be between teacher and student: student–student activity, in pairs or groups, also helps both reading and oral skills.

4 Sometimes you may want the students to write comprehension answers. If so, the students may need some assistance. It will probably be necessary to work through the questions orally first. In addition, one may have to rewrite the questions in the book, or devise different ones, e.g. as sentence-completion or blank-filling exercises – to ensure that the students perform satisfactorily.

5 The teacher, not the textbook writer, is the best judge of what follow-up activities are suitable for his or her particular class. These activities should develop both reading comprehension skills and communicative language use in an integrated manner. One activity – reading aloud – is best kept for dialogue.

6 Reading texts are often used not just for practising reading, but also for presenting new language. As a result, there may be too much 'textbookese' and not enough authentic reading material in a textbook. When this is the case, the teacher can bring authentic material in from outside the textbook. We shall look at some possibilities for finding authentic material in the next chapter.

7 Even in elementary classes, we can begin to foster more self-reliant attitudes to reading, as we saw in example 3.

Questions and activities

1 Make a list of the different kinds of reading text used in your textbook. Do you think that there is enough variety, a) in type? b) in subject matter?

2 Which of the reading texts in this chapter would you use with your students – and which would you prefer not to use? Suggest reasons for your answers.

3 Look at step 3 on page 66, and the Addendum on page 78. Is the teacher practising comprehension skills, oral language use, or both? Comment on the approach described on page 65.

4 Five different lesson plans are outlined on pages 65–67, all dealing with the reading passage on page 64. Which of these plans do you prefer, and why? If you like, draw up your own plan, selecting different steps from different plans.

5 What do you think of the lesson plan on page 70? Which of the variations listed on page 71 would you consider using, and why? In what steps in the lesson would you place each of these activities?

6 Draw up a detailed plan for step 2 of this lesson. Make up a suitable listening comprehension exercise to introduce the text.

7 Compare the first two texts, on pages 64 and 68, with the one on page 75. Which kind of text do you prefer, and why? Should a textbook have all three kinds of text, do you think?

8 Discuss the methods used for treating the *Ace Airlines* text on page 74. Are they appropriate for your students?
The book suggests this as a follow-up task:

Try to get the students to talk about their national airlines. Encourage them to say or communicate anything they can. You can use gentle correction, but avoid focussing on the students' accuracy (or lack of it).

What do you think of this fluency activity as a follow-up to this text?

9 Can you think of your own projective questions designed to get the students to respond to the text by talking about their own personal experience?

10 Apply the diagram on page 17 of this book to a reading text in your textbook. Draw up a mini-plan, using any of the approaches suggested in this chapter.

References

1 *English in Use Book 1* by N J H Grant and C R Wang'ombe, p 115 (Longman 1979)

2 *Access to English Book 1* (New Edition) by Michael Coles and
Basil Lord, p 123 (Oxford University Press 1984)
3 *Chuo English Studies Book 1* by M Ueyama and D C Tamaki,
p 33, 34 (Chuo Toshi 1984)
4 *Meridian Student's Book 1* by Jeremy Harmer, p 23 (Longman
1985) and *Teacher's Guide*, p 63.

Addendum

Oral questioning techniques

Here is part of a lesson showing how the teacher conducts oral questioning in a way the
textbook can't. What techniques does the teacher use to assist the students?

This is part of step 3 of the lesson on page 66. The reading passage referred to is on page 64.

T: What are double yellow lines? (Holds up piece of yellow chalk.) Who can draw double yellow lines for us?

S1: I miss!

T: Here you are, Tomas. (Tomas does so.) Good. What are these, class?

Ss: Duboo yerou rines.

T: No, listen: double yellow lines. (T and Ss repeat several times.)

T: What do they mean?

Ss: (Inaudible.)

T: What do double yellow lines mean in England?

S2: Edge of road.

T: Yes, the lines are at the edge of the road. What do they mean? (Several hands go up.) Alex!

S3: No parking.

T: Good! Yes, they mean no parking at any time. When did Arthur go to Swanage?

Ss: (Silence/inaudible.)

T: Can you remember? What day? (*Pause*) Did he go there on Monday?

S1: No.

T: Tuesday?

S4: Sunday, miss!

T: Is that right? Did they go to Swanage on Sunday?

Ss: Yes, miss, Sunday.

T: Can you park on double yellow lines on Sunday?

S5: Yes, miss.

T: Is that right? Is it allowed?

S6: No, no parking – no allowed!

T: Good! It's not allowed, at any time. Is it allowed on Saturday?

Ss: No, no parking!

T: Not allowed! Friday?

Ss: No!

T: Is parking allowed at any time?

Ss: No, no any time.

T: It's not allowed at any time. Repeat!

Ss: Not allowed at any time.

T: Good. So where was Arthur's car?

S7: Police have the car.

T: Yes, the police took the car. So where was it?

Ss: At police station.

T: Yes! It was at the police station. Why . . . (etc.)

Reading at intermediate and advanced levels

In this chapter we shall look at the teaching of reading at intermediate and advanced levels. At these levels, the students are still learning language content – grammar, vocabulary, idiom, etc. However, as one proceeds up the spiral staircase of language-learning, the emphasis increasingly falls on skills development. By this we mean both reading comprehension skills, and real-life skills that students need in real situations. The object is to enable the students to become increasingly self-reliant. At intermediate and advanced levels, many textbooks give advice on how the reading text should be handled, others leave it to you. In either case, it is our job as teachers to decide how to proceed.

Aims when using a reading text

We should always decide first what our aims are. These could be all or any of the following:

- to teach basic reading comprehension skills;
- to teach real-life reading skills such as reading for gist and reading for information;
- to develop flexible reading skills, varied according to purpose;
- to develop critical reading skills;
- to develop the students' knowledge of vocabulary or idiom;
- to reinforce (or even present) certain grammatical features;
- to act as a stimulus for oral or written work later on.

The textbook writer will have already decided which of the aims listed here are targeted for a particular reading exercise. It is for the teacher to decide which of these aims are appropriate in a particular lesson.

Textbooks may suffer from various deficiencies:

1 Very often, a textbook will neglect some of the aims listed on the last page. Aims 2, 3 and 4 are very frequently neglected. As a result, reading can all too often degenerate into a purely academic exercise, divorced from real life, and from the experience of the students.
2 Sometimes, a textbook will emphasise testing rather than training. Sometimes of course one may wish to test comprehension – but too many tests can mean too little teaching. Our students will suffer if this happens.
3 Sometimes a textbook will use the reading passage simply as a way of exposing the students to vocabulary. No genuine comprehension questions may be asked at all.
4 Sometimes the textbook asks inappropriate questions.

It is the teacher's job to make good these deficiencies, if and when they exist. Quite often the textbook might have missed opportunities that the teacher may spot, and take advantage of. While we may accept the aims given in the textbook, this does not prevent us from supplementing them as necessary or possible. We shall look at some examples of ways in which aims may be amended later in this chapter.

Methods for teaching reading

These may differ markedly from those recommended, or implied, in the textbook. Our methods will depend on our aims, and will focus on three aspects: how to present a text; how to develop a lesson using it; and how to follow it up.

1 Presenting a text

A good presentation can:

● arouse the students' interest;
● draw their attention to their own previous knowledge and experience, which will help them to attack the text;
● preteach any important words or concepts;
● give a reason for reading. This gives students a sense of purpose.

Above all, a good presentation should not be too long. Different texts will create different opportunities. Here are a few suggestions:

- Use a picture – in the book, or from another source – to get the students interested in the topic they are going to read about.
- Use the other senses where relevant. We should make much greater use in the classroom of the senses of taste, touch and smell, quite apart from sound. 'What do you think these noises are?' can be quite a good way of introducing a text!
- Ask pre-reading questions, to make the reading task more purposeful. For example, the text is about the Pyramids. In pairs, the students write down two lists – one of *Things we know about the Pyramids*, and one of *Things we aren't sure about*. They then read the text to see if they can fill in the gaps in their knowledge.
- Set a problem. The problem can be one based on a visual, for example, 'Look at this picture. Who are these people? What do you think they are doing? Read the text and find out.'
- Sometimes one can provide a problem in the form of an *information grid*. The students have to read a text and complete the blanks on their grid with information from the text.
- A listening exercise can be a good introduction, especially if it poses a problem which can be solved by reading a text.
- Get the students to preview a text to make it more predictable and therefore easier to understand. (See page 91 for more information about this.)

2 Developing the reading lesson

Again, we need to bear in mind our aims in planning the next stages in the lesson. We saw some of the things we can do to develop reading skills in the last chapter. We shall look at some further approaches in the examples in this chapter.

3 Follow-up

Again, this is best discussed in the context of particular reading passages. The main thing to remember is that a successful follow-up to a reading exercise involves integrating the language skills – especially speaking and writing. In this way reading and the other aspects of the syllabus are mutually reinforcing.

Example 1

In this first example,[1] you will see that the reading section is headed 'Understanding Descriptions'. As you read through it, consider these questions:

- How far is the heading an adequate description of the textbook writer's aims? Which question(s) help to achieve this aim?
- What other aims would you want to achieve if you were handling this exercise?
- How might you present this text to the class?

5.8 Understanding descriptions

Read these two newspaper reports and then answer the questions about them.

October 7th
Scientists in New Zealand are baffled by a 42-foot circle of dehydrated radioactive scrub found on farmland near Hamilton, North Island. The bushes show no sign of burning but experts believe they were instantly drained of all moisture and their
5 centres reduced to black carbon. Three V-shaped grooves forming a perfect triangle have been found imprinted in the ground inside the circle.

Mr John Stuart-Menzies, a leading New Zealand horticultural consultant, told reporters: 'Some object appears to have landed on
10 the spot and taken off, producing an energy which cooked the plants.' He said that some kind of short-wave high frequency radiation had cooked the plants instantaneously from the inside outwards – similar to the method used in infra-red cooking but on an enormous scale. He added: 'A meteorite or lightning could not
15 do this.'

Answer these questions about the report:

1 Why were the scientists baffled by the circle?
2 Suggest two reasons why Mr Stuart-Menzies thought that an object had landed on the spot and taken off.
3 Why did Mr Stuart-Menzies refer to a meteorite and lightning?
4 What effect do you think this report had on readers of the newspaper?
5 If you were a news editor and you received this report would you classify it as of (a) local, (b) national or (c) international interest?
6 Prepare a small sketch to illustrate the main point of the report. Draw the necessary sketch, as seen from above.

October 10th (Three days later, a further report appeared in newspapers on the same incident.)

The New Zealand Government employed nuclear scientists today to sweep away fears that flying saucers had landed on North Island. They investigated mysterious circles of bleached scrub that led to reports of radioactivity left by flying saucers and came up with the
20 answer: root rot.

Sightseers had flocked to an area near Hamilton, where a 42 ft diameter circle was found. The Science Minister, Mr Brian Talboys, examined a report made by Government nuclear scientists who analysed samples of the damaged scrub. He said that the
25 damage was not caused by extra-terrestial phenomena.

'The scrub has been affected by a root rot caused by organisms and blight,' he said. He pointed out that this type of root rot was not uncommon in New Zealand and that it often spread out from a central point to destroy plants within a circle.

---

1 Make up a suitable heading for the first news report.

2 In line 5 of the first report, what was the point of mentioning the grooves?

3 After studying both reports, what conclusion can you come to concerning the accuracy of the first report of the grooves?

4 Why did the reporters speak to Mr Stuart-Menzies?

5 Give two ways in which the people in New Zealand apparently reacted when they read the first report.

6 What did Mr Stuart-Menzies probably think when he read the second report?

In questions 7 to 12, choose the most suitable answer.

7 Which of these words best describes the nature of the first report?
A scientific
B speculative
C geographical
D biological

8 Which word in the first report shows that Mr Stuart-Menzies was not absolutely certain what had happened?
A appears
B energy
C cooked
D enormous

9 Which expression in the first report explains the meaning of 'dehydrated' (in line 2)?
A no sign of burning
B reduced to black carbon
C forming a perfect triangle
D drained of all moisture

10 When officials of the New Zealand Government read the first report, they apparently
A ignored it
B believed it
C thought it was amusing
D took it seriously

11 We may conclude from the second report that
A Mr Talboys was a scientist interested in nuclear matters
B people were not very interested in the first report
C no flying saucers actually landed in New Zealand
D the plants destroyed the root rot when they made a circle

12 In line 17, 'sweep away' is similar in meaning to
A purity
B get rid of
C make clean
D prove the truth of

5.9 Word study

1 Discuss in class the difference between 'baffled' and 'puzzled' in these two sentences:
a) Scientists in New Zealand are *baffled* by a 42-foot circle of scrub.
b) Scientists in New Zealand are *puzzled* by a 42-foot circle of scrub.

2 What differences in usage do you notice in these expressions?
a) a 42-foot circle; a six foot snake;
b) a circle with a diameter of 42 feet; a snake six feet long.

3 What does scrub look like?

4 What is the use, function or purpose of 'perfect' in line 6?

5 Do you think there is any difference in meaning between 'instantly' in line 4 and 'instantaneously' in line 12? If so, what is the difference?

6 Name any bleaching (line 18) agent available in Malaysian shops.

7 What does 'flocked' mean in line 21?

8 Where would 'extra-terrestial phenomena' come from?

9 Of the two words 'effect' and 'affect', which occurs more commonly as a noun, and which is more often used as a verb?

Although only one aim seems to be stated in the textbook – that of understanding descriptions, clearly other aims are targeted, too, including these:

● practising plain sense and deductive reading skills;
● developing vocabulary.

Both of these aims appear to be valid as far as they go. However, we can use this exercise to achieve other aims as well, including at least this one:

● developing critical, projective, reading skills.

These texts raise some interesting questions about life on other planets which they do not really answer. Here then is good material for thought and argument – just what we want in our language class. One suggested approach which provides for this appears below. Before looking at the suggested approach, you may like to consider how *you* might handle these two texts.

Approach A	1 Presentation. Pre-teach/revise key vocabulary as necessary, including *flying saucer* and *extra-terrestial*, using visuals such as a picture from the film *E.T.* Give this question to students for the first text: 'Read this newspaper report as quickly as you can, and suggest a suitable headline.' Students read the text quickly, suggested headlines are discussed, and the best written on the board.
	2 Get students to read the text again more carefully, to find out the answers to Q 1–3. Treat vocabulary incidentally.
	3 Discuss their answers, and Q 4–6. Also ask this important question: 'You've read the evidence in the first report – what do you think?'
	4 Set this pre-question, and get students to read the second report as quickly as they can: 'Does the second news report change your opinion after reading the first report. If so why?'
	5 Discuss the students' answers, and these questions: a) the second Q 5; b) Is the explanation given by the government scientist completely satisfactory? If not, why not?
	6 Students write individual answers to Q 7–12 in number-letter form. The teacher collects them in for marking.
	7 Discuss the word study section as necessary. Also these two projective questions: 'Do you believe in flying saucers?'; 'Do you think that there is life on other planets?'

Comments on Approach A

General comments

In general, we can say that Approach A is suitable if you are short of time. Its aims are as described on the previous page. The approach differs from that of the book in several respects:

a) It aims at developing critical reading;

b) Its presentation differs considerably from the one line rubric of the students' book. See for example the pre-reading questions before each text, which are particularly important;

c) It asks different questions, and some of the book's questions, in a different order and in a manner designed to encourage the readers to think;

d) The lesson ends, not with the rather uninteresting 'word study' exercise, but with two questions designed to encourage the students to express themselves orally in English.

Detailed comments

1 The question in step 1 is designed to get the students to understand the main points of the story, and sum them up in a headline.

2 The questions: teachers will have their own ideas on which of the questions in the book to ask, and in what order. In this case, the questions in stages 3 and 4 are not in the book, and are crucial in developing critical reading.

3 In this approach the students must be given the opportunity for silent reading. It is best to get them to do this at least twice – once as a fast preliminary read, and once more carefully, to find out the answers to some or all of the questions in the book.

4 Note the projective questions in step 7 of the lesson. These are not examination-type questions. But they are valid and important, and arise naturally from a reading of these texts. Students who have not thought about such issues cannot really be said to have read these texts more than superficially.

What follow-up activities do you think might be appropriate?

5 Notice that in Approach A, there is no allowance for any follow-up activities. However, such activities could be done in a later lesson, and help to integrate the reading exercise with other areas of the English syllabus – in this case, speechwork and writing skills.

Now let us look at Approach B:

Approach B	Steps 1–4 as above.
	5 Students write individual answers to Q 7–12, and the teacher collects them in for marking.
	6 Discussion groups: the students get into groups of 4 or 5, and discuss their answers to Q 7–12, and this question, written on the board: 'Is the explanation given by the government scientists completely satisfactory?'
	7 Class discussion of group answers, and of word study questions. Also: 'Do you believe in flying saucers? Do you think there is life on another planet?'
	8 Role-play: Get students to write down the questions they would like to ask the Science Minister. Interview of the Minister.
	9 A purposeful writing exercise, for example, blank-filling summary of the two reports for a newspaper, or writing a letter to a newspaper.

Comments on Approach B

General comments

The aims remain the same, except that this lesson has these two additional aims:

a) to give practice in oral communication;

b) to develop writing (or summary) skills.

This lesson would probably take at least twice as long as the previous one. Its distinctive features include those already listed for Approach A, and:

c) group discussion of the questions;

d) role-play;

e) written work.

Detailed comments

1 Steps 5, 6 and 7: It is often suggested that multiple-choice questions are suitable only for testing. Here the teacher collected in the students' answers for marking – but then used the questions, not just to *test* the students, but to *train* them. The approach used here shows how students can be required to think out their answers, and justify them to their fellow students. Thus reading and thinking skills are integrated with speechwork.[2]

2 Steps 8 and 9 indicate ways in which reading can be integrated with, and used as a stimulus for, other activities.

Real-life reading skills

So far, our discussion in this chapter has focussed mainly on developing the basic reading skills and integrating them with other aspects of English, such as speechwork and writing. However, our teaching should also cater for encouraging *real-life* reading skills, too. In general terms, there are three skills that should concern us:

● reading for gist;

● reading for information;

● reading for study.

It is important to note that textbooks do not always provide for these real-life reading skills. This need not prevent us from doing the job, however. Even reading texts that are not used in the textbook to develop such skills may be used for this purpose.

These skills are needed to achieve a great variety of different purposes. To teach these skills effectively, we need to know what reading purposes our students have, or are likely to have, in real life. In addition, since we frame our reading purposes before we read, and not after, it is important that any purposeful reading should be preceded by *pre-reading questions*, as we have seen. These help the students to read purposefully. Let us examine each of these skills in turn.

1 Reading for gist

This means reading to get the main point or points of a text. Reading for gist is a very common form of reading, most frequent perhaps in reading a newspaper, although it is also a useful study skill. The 'Naked Truth' text in the last chapter offered a good example of this skill. Our purpose in reading the text was to satisfy our curiosity, and so we were likely to want to read it quite quickly, to get the gist of the story.

Example 2

Look at the text on the next page.[3]
1) What reading skills does it practise?
2) Does it approach the text in a true-to-life manner, or a classroom manner?
As you see, this interesting magazine extract is followed by fairly traditional language-learning exercises. These exercises are of course valid: they are no doubt a necessary part of the learning programme – or, at least, of the examination programme. The question is, are they sufficient? Wouldn't our students appreciate it if such texts were used, not just as classroom exercises, but as communicative exercises which link up with real life? Consider how we might do this before reading on.

The main difference between a classroom reading text and a real-life reading text is that the latter requires a reading purpose. There is seldom or never a genuine reading purpose in the classroom (unlike real life). So it is up to the teacher to suggest a plausible one. This usually requires making a context for reading – just as one tries to provide a context for oral language practice. One possible task for students is outlined on page 90.

UNIT 1

HOMES

Reading and thinking
Reading comprehension (1)

Setting up home

When Fred Giffin bought his three-storey unconverted Victorian house under the GLC Homesteading scheme, the property market was very different from what it is now.

'There were queues in estate agents' on Saturday mornings,' recalls Fred, 'and competition between buyers was fierce.'

'All I wanted,' sighs Fred, 'was a house in Highbury, North London. As I am a decorator and have got friends in the building trade, the condition of the property was unimportant. I was optimistic that I'd be able to convert almost anything.'

What Fred did not realise was the huge amount of money he would have to spend, and the time it would take. He and his wife Mercia and their three children were due to move in six months after buying but they finally moved in eighteen months ago, and the house is still far from finished.

The back extension had to be demolished, and the whole house had to be replumbed and rewired, and fitted with new drains. Fred was also keen to restore original features. 'I have seen so many conversions,' he emphasises, 'where the builders rip out all the good bits – the shutters and pine doors – only to use cheap, modern materials instead.' But knowing what's thrown out with the rubbish can be useful: he said that shutters make very good cupboard doors when cut into three, and he rescued some old iron railings from his garden.

But Fred admits he was very ambitious. 'I was not interested in reselling the house at the time. I was doing it up to keep, so I wanted the work done properly. If I'd been after a "builder's finish" the house would have been completed in half the time.'

He hired an architect and, because he is a perfectionist himself, wanted to find the right person for the right job. 'Because I am in the building trade myself,' he explains, 'I am aware of the low standard of work, and I would advise anyone who needs a builder to try and see his work first. If his own house is decent then it follows that his work should be of a similar standard.'

He asked a friend of his to estimate the work. Although it seemed a lot at the time, £25,000 was more or less correct. 'It's like turning on a tap,' says Fred, 'when it comes to doing up old houses. You have no idea how much things are going to cost until you start. I made a series of expensive mistakes – which I now regret.

'I wanted to do things by the book,' he adds. 'I made sure that all the walls were lined to eliminate dust and dirt. I restored cornices and put back fireplaces. But even now the kitchen still hasn't been decorated, and the utility room hasn't been started.'

Asked about any future plans, Fred expressed a desire to move sometime. Although the house is convenient for public transport, its proximity to Arsenal Stadium means a noisy Saturday afternoon. Given the choice again Fred would like to be in a quieter street, with a bigger garden, and fewer rooms to decorate. With four years' work behind him, Fred is ready for a rest. 'You only learn the hard way,' he says, but his advice to anyone buying old property is to have a healthy bank balance and lots of energy!

Buying and Improving your Home
August 1983

---

1 Which of the following statements are true and which are false? Put ticks (√) by the statements that are true and give reasons for your answers.

a The Giffins moved in six months after buying the house. ☐

b Fred wanted to use cheap, modern materials. ☐

c Fred probably cut up some shutters that had been thrown out. ☐

d Fred always planned to sell the house later. ☐

e It would have been possible to convert the house twice as quickly. ☐

f Fred thinks that building work is usually of poor quality. ☐

g It took four years to complete the conversion. ☐

For questions 2 to 4 choose the phrase which best completes each sentence.

2 The property market has changed in that
   a estate agents' now close on Saturday mornings.
   b buyers used to fight each other fiercely.
   c not so many people are interested in buying houses now.
   d not so many people are interested in selling houses now.

3 The £25,000 estimate made by a friend
   a was for the cost of the water supply.
   b was an expensive mistake.
   c made Fred regret his plans.
   d was what the conversion actually cost in the end.

4 Fred wanted to do the conversion
   a according to the instructions in a book.
   b as thoroughly as possible.
   c in the same way that a real builder would do it.
   d in order to learn how to be a builder.

5 Write a summary explaining what, according to the article, were the advantages and disadvantages of buying this particular house.

Imagine that your cousin is thinking of buying a house in your town. He can't afford a lot of money, so he hopes to be able to buy an older one and modernise it himself. Read this article as quickly as you can, and find the three problems he might have to face.

This approach has several advantages:
- it gives the students a purpose for the exercise;
- it trains them to read quickly for gist: if they can answer this question, they have got the gist of the article;
- it will encourage interested talk about real-life issues;
- it helps to prepare the students for other useful language activities later. (For example, you might want to ask them to write to the cousin, giving him some advice on his proposed house purchase.)

This type of question can be asked before any textbook reading passage – though obviously some texts are more suitable than others. If your textbook does not ask such pre-reading questions, then it is a good idea to do so yourself. In fact, almost any text can be preceded by either a 'reading for gist' question, or a 'reading for information' question, which we shall now discuss.

2 Reading for information

Reading for information is another very important skill. It is different from reading for gist, because it requires the reader to read selectively – to find or choose those parts of the text that are relevant. Examples include looking up a telephone number, or a word in the dictionary, finding out travel times, consulting a catalogue, and looking something up in an encyclopedia.

Example 3

In this example on page 91,[4] the students have an extract from a book of records (like the famous *Guinness Book of Records*). They have to find out the answers to some questions as quickly as possible. (This could even be in the form of a competition.) Here are some sample questions:
1 What was the weight of the largest land mammal on record?
2 Which is heavier – an adult whale, or an adult elephant?
3 Which country will have a higher population in the year 2,000 – India or China?

Facts and figures

Which is the biggest animal in the world?
The largest and heaviest animal that has
ever lived is the blue whale. The biggest
ever recorded weighed 190 tonnes. The blue
whale can grow to more than 33 metres in
length.

The largest land animal is the African
elephant. The largest specimen on record is
a bull elephant shot in southern Angola in
1974. This elephant was 3.96 metres in
height, and weighed about 12.24 tonnes.

Which is the longest-living mammal?
No mammal lives for longer than man.
According to the *Guinness Book of Records*,
the record is held by Shigechiyo Izumi of
Japan, who was born on 29 June 1865, and
who was alive and well on his 119th
birthday. In his opinion, the best way to a
long life is 'not to worry', and to leave
things to 'God, the Sun and Buddha'.

Which country has the biggest population?
The people's Republic of China has the
largest population in the world. According
to the census of July 1982, China had a
population of over a billion – 1,008,175,288.
China is now very anxious to control its
population, and has introduced radical
policies with the aim of stabilising its
population at about 1.2 billion by the year
2,000. On present trends, India will overtake
China sometime in the twenty-first century.

Marriage ages
The lowest average ages for marriage are in
India, with 20.0 years for males, and 14.5 for
females. The highest average ages are in
Ireland, with 31.4 for males, and 26.5 for
females.

In China, the recommended age for
marriage for men is 28, and for women 25.

3 Reading for study

This is necessary in any situation where our students may have to
study texts in other subjects in the English language. A detailed
account of this element in the reading programme is beyond the
scope of this book, but a few general comments may be helpful.

Previewing a text

This skill is extremely valuable – and not just in study situations.
Previewing (or surveying) a text is rather like looking at a map
before beginning a journey. It involves making a text easier to
understand by making it more predictable. We don't need any
special textbooks, or other materials, to practise this skill.
Previewing the text involves these operations before reading a text
in detail:

- looking at any introductory material there may be;
- looking at any illustrations or diagrams (and the captions);
- looking at headings and subheadings, if any;
- reading the first paragraph, and (typically, but not always) the first sentence of each of the other paragraphs;
- reading the last paragraph.

An efficient study method: P3RU

This involves five stages:

P – PREVIEW the reading text in the manner suggested above;

R – READ the text carefully;

R – RECORD the main points of the text in note form;

R – REVIEW or REVISE: read through the text again, quite quickly. Find out the answers to any questions you have – e.g. anything you didn't understand. Amend your notes as necessary.

U – USE the information you have obtained from the text, both in discussion with your friends, and in writing (e.g. an essay).

There are many variations on P3RU. If these skills are needed by your students, and are not handled in your textbook, you should find a supplementary book. The alternative is to devise exercises based on P3RU, using what other subject textbooks your students have. Note that you should always consult with your colleagues in other subjects when planning this kind of work.

Summary

1 In this chapter we have seen that at intermediate and advanced levels, textbooks frequently neglect important aims such as real-life reading skills, flexible reading for different purposes, and critical reading skills. When this is the case, teachers should look for opportunities of achieving such aims, and should also adjust their methods of approach.

2 Many textbooks rely on the teacher to present a reading exercise in a way that will excite the interest of the students. At this stage, it is very important to involve the students personally, so that the reading text links up with their own experience.

3 We should pay particular attention to the nature and type of questions the textbook contains and be prepared to add to, amend, re-order or omit them, to achieve the aims that we have decided on. Projective questions, which require the students to react personally to the text, should not be neglected.

4 Appropriate activities at these levels include the setting in advance of a variety of different purposes for reading such as group discussions, and jigsaw reading – in fact, any activity which gives a purpose for reading.

5 Reading should not be treated as an isolated skill; a good text should lead to work in other areas, including vocabulary development, speechwork, summary work, etc.

Questions and activities

1 Look at the reading aims listed on page 79. Can you think of any others? Which of these aims are well-covered in the textbook you are using, and which are not so well-covered? What can you do about it?

2 Look at any one of the texts in your textbook. Can you think of an interesting way of presenting it?

3 Look at the group discussion method used in Approach B on page 86 again. List the advantages and disadvantages of this method. Why not try it out with one of your classes, to see how it goes?

4 Look at your textbook. Does it concentrate on reading for gist, reading for information, or reading for study? Which of these skills are required by your students? Consider how you might teach these skills, using your textbook.

5 Consider the study method 'P3RU'. Do you think you would find this relevant and useful? How might you adapt it for your own purposes?

References

1 *Communication Skills in English* by A R B Etherton, sections 5.8, 5.9 (Longman Malaysia 1976)

2 See *Read and Think* by J L Munby (Longman 1979)

3 *Options* by M Hinton and R Marsden, p 1, 2 (Nelson 1986)

4 *English for Zimbabwe Book 1* by N J H Grant and H Ndanga, p 95 (Longman Zimbabwe 1986)

Writing skills at elementary level

Why do we wish to teach our students to write? There are two main objectives:

- to enable the students to respond appropriately in writing in those situations that require it;
- to enable the students to consolidate their knowledge of the language.

For most beginners, the situations when they have to use the written forms of the language will still seem fairly remote at this stage. So while some of the most effective writing exercises will be those that may appear realistic or authentic, in practice their purpose will be nearer the second objective than the first.

Let us look more closely at the second objective. To many learners, new language is not really properly learned until they have written it down. This is why, in lessons that are predominantly oral, students will jot down notes whenever they can during the lesson. We may have our own good reasons for having oral lessons, but it is important to meet learners' needs halfway. So if they think they need to write something down occasionally, let them!

The mini-exercise

A mini-exercise could be called 'a controlled jotting', and seldom appears in a textbook. A mini-exercise usually arises from a classroom situation when either the teacher, or the students, may suddenly feel the need for it. It consolidates, and reassures. 'Yes, it's simple, you've got it down on paper!' the teacher seems to say, as there is a pause for the mini-exercise.

Unless they are supervised, students will tend to jot down all sorts of garbled language, full of inaccuracies and spelling mistakes. Teachers can ensure that what students write down is useful and accurate by giving a mini-exercise.

Let us look at an example. The teacher has been practising the difference between *bring* and *take*. Students always like to make a note of new words, if only on the back of an envelope, or in a corner of their exercise book. So it is a good idea for the teacher to make sure that they do so neatly and accurately. The most functional way of doing this is by making sure they illustrate their use in context:

bring: Everyday I bring my books to school.
take: The teacher takes my books home for marking.

These are not particularly exciting sentences – yet they do their job very well: the use of these two verbs could not be clearer. The teacher gets them to write down these sentences in the back of their exercise books. (Some prefer to keep special vocabulary notebooks.) Getting the students to write sample sentences like these neatly in their books is far better than allowing them to make random untidy and inaccurate notes on scrap paper.

With younger or even older learners, the writing can be accompanied by drawings. For example:

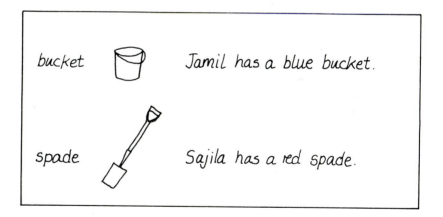

The writing exercises in the textbook

Of course, the textbook will usually contain a great many exercises of one kind or another. In some textbooks these may be very traditional. Such textbooks may contain exercises consisting of 5, or 10 numbered sentences, each with a blank. These are copied out, their blanks filled in, marked – and forgotten. Here is an example.

Example 1:
a traditional
exercise

> Choose the correct verb for these sentences:
>
> | | | | |
> |---|---|---|---|
> | 1 Sergio always . . . hard. | | arrive | catches |
> | 2 Ali usually . . . late. | | works | change |
> | 3 Sophie usually . . . the early bus. | | miss | use |
> | 4 Yasmin does not . . . her uniform at home. | | arrives | changes |

There are many variations on this kind of exercise, including blank-filling, sentence-completion, and translation exercises. How should we do this sort of exercise if it appears in a textbook which we are required to use? Here are some ideas.

- Omit it! We should certainly consider this possibility. Such exercises bear little relationship to the way language is used in real life, and are very boring. So it is better if we can think of ways of practising writing such sentences in a more realistic manner. We shall look at possible ways of doing this later. But first, here are some other things one can do with the traditional exercise:
- Amend the sentences in the exercise so that they are more relevant to your students. This kind of exercise can easily be rewritten on the board, so that the names of real students and situations familiar to the class are used.
- Adapt the exercise to make it easier. If the textbook has an exercise like the one above, and you think it is too hard, you can make it easier in various ways. For example, the appropriate verb for each sentence could be put in its infinitive form in brackets at the end of the sentence, or you could get the students to do the exercise orally in pairs first.
- You could make the exercise harder by not listing the verbs, and making the students think up suitable verbs themselves. This could also be done in pairs.
- Change the exercise. For example, you could make it a 'jumbled word' exercise. Sentence 4 might appear like this:
  4 uniform home. Her change not Yasmin does at

Testing and training

There is one thing that we should make clear at this point: is our purpose to test, or to train? Most traditional exercises, like the one we have just been looking at, are more appropriate in an examination or test. They can be marked quickly and easily, and can be aimed at testing the students' knowledge of particular areas of the language – in this case, the present simple tense.

However, most of the time in the classroom we want to train, not test. We much prefer our students to get things right – and so do they. This is the case especially with writing. Accuracy in writing is usually considered quite important. This is because something inaccurately written down can all too easily be absorbed by the learner.

In this chapter we shall assume that the aim is to teach, not test. Once we are clear about this, we can adopt a much more interesting approach to the teaching of writing skills. Writing is no longer something that students do on their own, to provide marks for the mark book. An exercise, even of the most traditional kind, can be done by students in pairs and in this way they practise both speaking and writing.

Example 2

In this example,[1] the textbook writer has included homework exercises in the students' textbook. Here is one of the exercises. Such exercises done by the students on their own are, in effect, tests. How would you handle these exercises in your class?

C George comes from Wales. He is twenty-four years old. Now he lives near Oxford. He works at a bookshop in the centre of Oxford. He sells old books and he knows a lot about them. He is tall and slim and he has dark hair and brown eyes. He writes about old books for a magazine called *Rare Books*.

1 Ask where George comes from.
2 Ask how old he is.
3 Ask where he lives.
4 Ask where he works.
5 Ask what he sells.
6 Ask what colour his eyes are.
7 Ask what he writes about.
8 Ask what magazine he writes for.

Now ask questions about George.

D Write answers to your questions about George.

Exercise C might usefully be done in class first, as an oral activity. If your class is not used to pairwork, you should organise a demonstration pair first. This might go as follows:

TEACHER: Claudio, Ricardo, take it in turns to ask the question. You first, Ricardo. Where does . . .

RICARDO: Er, where George, er, where does George come from?

CLAUDIO: George, um, he come from, er, Wales.

TEACHER: Good. Claudio, don't say George, say he.

CLAUDIO: He come – comes – from Wales.

TEACHER: Good. Now you ask the question, Claudio.

CLAUDIO: How old he is – um, er, how old is he?

RICARDO: George – he – is twenty-four years old.

TEACHER: Question 3 – Ricardo!

RICARDO: Where he – um, where does he live? (etc.)

The students now practise the same exercise in pairs, each student answering one question, and then asking the next. The teacher supervises. This exercise acts as oral revision, and is also a preparation for the writing exercise. The teacher tries to encourage accuracy as well as fluency, in the hope that the students will write the exercise more accurately, too. At the end of the session, the teacher can list the commonest errors the students have made, and warn them against them in the writing exercise. The students are then ready to do exercises C and D on their own.

Personalising exercises

Example 3

The best writing results are obtained when learners write about themselves and their own experiences. These activities come in a unit called 'What's your address?'[2] Exercises like this immediately seem much more purposeful and interesting to the learner.

3 Work in pairs. Ask and answer the questions.	**4 Copy and complete.**
What's your address?	My name is . . .
What's your telephone number?	I am . . . years old.
How old are you?	My address is . . .
What's your favourite number?	My telephone number is . . .
	My favourite number is . . .

Parallel writing

Example 4

One way of personalising their writing is by giving the students a text, and then asking them to construct one on similar lines about themselves. This can be done at quite a low level. Here, for example, is an exercise[3] which practises the present simple tense. This kind of exercise is a much more interesting way of practising writing skills than the exercise we looked at in example 1 on page 96.

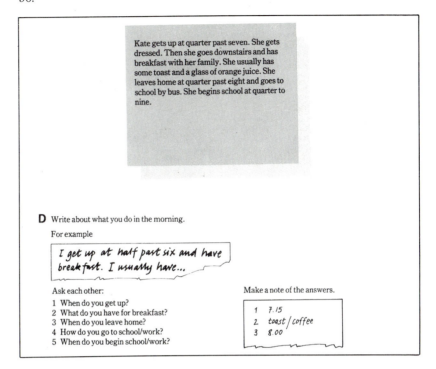

> Kate gets up at quarter past seven. She gets dressed. Then she goes downstairs and has breakfast with her family. She usually has some toast and a glass of orange juice. She leaves home at quarter past eight and goes to school by bus. She begins school at quarter to nine.

D Write about what you do in the morning.

For example

I get up at half past six and have breakfast. I usually have...

Ask each other:
1 When do you get up?
2 What do you have for breakfast?
3 When do you leave home?
4 How do you go to school/work?
5 When do you begin school/work?

Make a note of the answers.

1 7.15
2 toast / coffee
3 8.00

Although speechwork is a useful *preparation* for writing, useful speechwork can also *follow* writing. In this case, the students' own writing is the basis for an information-gap exercise. This leads to note-making by one student on another's answers. The students' writing thus not only gives them useful writing practice based on the parallel text above, but it also leads into classroom activities in which students talk about their own experiences.

Information-gap exercises

In example 1, we saw writing for its own sake: there was no purpose, and the information contained in the sentences was of minimal value or use. In contrast, in the last example, we saw that the information contained in the writing exercise was of central interest to the students because it was about themselves. A great deal of writing at the beginners' level can arise out of speechwork exercises in which students exchange information about themselves. Here is one last example.

Example 5

Step 15, below is a listening and speaking exercise practising certain adjectival patterns.[4] This leads into step 16, which is done in pairs. The writing exercise follows directly out of this information-gap exercise:

Making up writing exercises

Some textbooks do not include enough suitable writing exercises. If you have a textbook that falls into this category, you may have to make up appropriate exercises yourself. We have already seen some of the types of exercise that you can construct in this chapter. Before looking at some other examples, the following should be noted:

What makes a good writing exercise?

- Writing exercises should be neither too hard nor too easy. As a rough guide, they should be sufficiently hard to give the students a sense of achievement – and sufficiently easy for them to be able to take some pride in the result.
- Writing exercises should be relevant, both to the students, and to the subject dealt with in the unit of learning. A good writing exercise should arise naturally out of the other activities in the unit of work.
- They should be linguistically suitable, both in terms of grammar and vocabulary. This means that an exercise should consolidate vocabulary and should also revise grammatical structures the students have recently been learning to use.
- Writing exercises should not be too long.
- They should be interesting in their own right. In other words, what is written should have some kind of communicative purpose. A communicative writing exercise can have three different kinds of purpose:

  1 *functional.* An example of this might be a note to one's teacher apologising for missing a lesson;
  2 *personal* – such as writing about oneself, one's best friend, or one's family;
  3 *imaginative.* In this case, the subject might be so interesting that the students don't mind the fact that there is no definite personal or functional aim, other than using the language in an interesting context.

  We shall look at these three kinds of purposeful writing in the next few examples.

Writing for a purpose: (1) functional

It is a good idea for the teacher to compile a list of all the situations in which the students might conceivably be involved in writing activities either in the present or in the forseeable future. This is not always easy, of course; but even situations which are just about imaginable are better than no situations at all – when one is reduced to exercises like the one in example 1. Often, we hope, the syllabus will do this job – but if it doesn't, then it's up to the teacher.

Opportunities include:

- writing to pen friends;
- writing to the teacher for some reason or other, such as apologising for one's absence;
- writing down information about local places or events for a foreign visitor.

Perhaps you can think of some other ideas. Let us look at just two examples.

Example 6 This exercise is devised by the teacher and the material is from a tourist's brochure on Vienna. The situation is that an American boy is spending two weeks as a visitor in your school (which is in Vienna). He needs some local information about places to visit, where to eat, how to travel around the city, etc. Local tourist brochures will provide plenty of information you can adapt for classroom use. You could devise the following cloze exercise. ('Cloze' basically means 'gap-filling'.)

Step 1 Explain the situation.
Step 2 Issue handouts – one between two will do.
Step 3 In pairs, students discuss the sheets, and decide on how they would complete the blanks.
Step 4 Class follow-up discussion. Different suggestions are compared, final answers decided on, and put on the board.
Step 5 Answers are rubbed out. Students write individual answers.

Getting around Vienna
When sightseeing, it is best to . . . (1) . . . a 72-hour ticket. This ticket . . . (2) . . . only 92 Austrian schillings. You can get . . . (3) . . . tickets from different . . . (4) . . . , including public transport information points, railway . . . (5) . . . , tobacconists and official . . . (6) . . . information offices. Before you . . . (7) . . . your first journey, write your full . . . (8) . . . in the space on the ticket.

Example 7 Our second example of functional writing is more difficult to devise. However, it can also be treated as a pair activity, and it also leads to the students producing a near-perfect piece of writing. The students are asked to do this worksheet in pairs, deciding which versions they prefer. Notice that they can make up their own words at various points in the letter. Later, they can write out their own version, making whichever choices they like.

Dear (teacher)

I am very sorry that I did not   come to class   yesterday. do my homework   last week. . . .   . . .

My brother had an accident, and I went to the hospital. I was not well, and went to the doctor. . . . .

Please   accept my apologies for my absence. allow me a little extra time. . . . .

Yours sincerely (signature)

This kind of exercise can be done in many different ways, and has many variations. There is no reason why every letter should be addressed to the teacher – students can write to each other as well. Obviously, such letters are not possible until they have made a start on the simple past tense, but once they have done this exercise, they can be asked to write a letter like this every time they miss class, or fail to do their homework on time!

Writing for a purpose: (2) personal

Example 8

This kind of exercise may not have a genuine function at all. But it is still purposeful, because, people being what they are, writing (or talking!) about themselves is purpose enough.

This exercise is a more interesting example of parallel writing than we had before (example 2), and starts off with an interesting reading exercise in which students have to fill in the details about Gisela.[5] (This task could be done in pairs if desired.)

The students then simply rewrite the letter in any way that makes it true for them. Of course, it is even better if the letter can be to a genuine pen friend.

Reading

WANTED PENFRIENDS

French boy 15, wants penfriends from all over the world. Please write in English. Likes sports, films, pop music. Write to Jean Ploton Box 234

10 Trafalgar Road,
Bolihull,
Birmingham.
10th March, 198.

Dear Jean,
   Hello! I'm seventeen years old. I'm German and I'm a student. I study in Birmingham.
   I like reading, writing letters and going to the cinema, but I don't like cooking! I speak English, German and a little French. I like sports very much, too. I love windsurfing in the summer. Can you windsurf? It's great fun!
   Write soon.
      Gisela (Hanz)
P.S. I don't smoke. Do you?

Fill in the details about Gisela:

Full name:	
Address:	
Age:	
Nationality:	
Likes:	
Dislikes:	
Sports:	
Languages:	

Writing
Write a similar letter to Jean and tell him about yourself.

34

Writing for a purpose: (3) imaginative

Example 9

Even with beginners, it is possible to devise interesting exercises that can capture their imagination, and help them to enjoy the process of language-learning. This example is based on a course we looked at earlier in this book.[6] The course is primarily oral in the opening stages, and most of the writing tasks suggested in it are dictation exercises. There is therefore scope for teachers to bring in writing ideas of their own whenever they feel this to be appropriate. In this case, all the activities in the unit are oral.

30 I want you, Fiona

Charles Please marry me, Fiona. I want you, I need you, I love you.

Fiona I'm sorry Charles, but I can't.

Charles Oh, Fiona. Why not?

Fiona Well, Charles. I like you . . . I like you a lot . . . but I don't love you.

Charles But Fiona, love isn't everything.

Fiona Oh, Charles, you don't understand . . . for me love is everything.

Charles Do you love another man Fiona?

Fiona Yes Charles, I do . . . James.

Charles Not James Milton!

Fiona Yes, James Milton.

Charles But he doesn't want you. He's engaged.

Fiona I know.

Charles But Fiona, James isn't a rich man. I can give you everything. What do you want? Clothes? Money? Travel? A big house?

Fiona No, Charles. I don't want those things. I only want James.

Questions

Who wants Fiona?
Does he love her?
Does Fiona like Charles?
Does she like him a lot?
Does she love him?
Does Fiona love another man?
What's his name?
Does James want Fiona?
Is he rich?
Is Charles rich?
What can he give Fiona?
Does she want clothes?
Does she want money?
What does she want?

Exercise 1

Who wants Fiona?
Charles wants Fiona.

Who loves Fiona?
Who needs Fiona?
Who wants James?
Who loves James?

Exercise 2

Who does Charles want?
Charles wants Fiona.

Who does Charles love?
Who does Fiona love?
Who does Fiona want?
Who does Charles need?

This amusing unit could be followed by a cloze exercise consisting of an incomplete letter from Charles to a newspaper Agony Aunt, Lucy, who writes a column called 'Letters to Lucy' in a newspaper:

> Dear Lucy
>
> Please help me. I . . . (1) . . . a beautiful girl called Fiona, but she . . . (2) . . . me. She says that she . . . (3) . . . a man called James Milton. But James is already engaged to another woman. Fiona . . . (4) . . . that he is already engaged, but still . . . (5) . . . to marry him.
>
> I am not a poor man. I can . . . (6) . . . Fiona anything – clothes, money, a big house, anything. Fiona says she . . . (7) . . . these things. She says she . . . (8) . . . me a lot, but she . . . (9) . . . me. She . . . (10) . . . only one thing – love.
>
> I . . . (11) . . . what to do. Please . . . (12) . . . me.
>
> Yours sincerely,
>
> Charles Arbuthnot
>
> Use the correct verbs in the blanks:
>
> | give | love | doesn't want | loves | knows | doesn't love |
> | wants | likes | doesn't love | help | wants | don't know |

This exercise is intended partly to practise the present simple tense. It also gives useful practice in distinguishing between *love*, *like* and *want*. The exercise illustrates one way in which a teacher could imaginatively supplement this unit of work in the textbook. There are several ways this exercise could be treated:

1 The students work in pairs, to come up with the right answer. Good classes would not be given the list of words at the end. Once the answers have been discussed in class, the students write the letter.
2 Later, of course, some students may like to write Lucy's reply to Charles Arbuthnot.
3 Alternatively, perhaps some of the students may like to compose Fiona's letter to Lucy – and the Agony Aunt's reply!

Summary

1 Writing should be done 'a little and often'. Many successful exercises are quite short mini-exercises devised by the teacher to

give students the chance to consolidate their learning. These exercises, like all writing exercises, should be integrated with the other skills, so that the writing can reinforce the other syllabus aims.

2 Many textbooks contain very traditional exercises which practise the forms of language in a meaningless way, devoid of any context. These exercises can be done in a more interesting way, perhaps, but usually they can be replaced with other more relevant exercises.

3 Testing exercises are often mistaken for teaching exercises: our priority is to teach. One useful approach is to help students to help each other by working through exercises in pairs orally before writing. This often minimises the chances of error.

4 When devising writing exercises we should try to personalise them wherever possible: this means they should appeal to the students' own personal experience. One way of doing this is parallel writing.

5 Another way of making writing interesting is by ensuring that it has interesting content or information. We can then use students' writing as a basis for information-gap exercises in which they find out information from each other.

6 In making up exercises, we should bear in mind the characteristics they should have (see page 101).

7 The best writing exercises have a purpose other than merely that of language practice. Suitable exercises can be devised even for beginners. They include exercises with: functional purposes (e.g. letters of apology, summaries of useful information); personal purposes (e.g. telling a pen friend about oneself); and imaginative purposes (the sky's the limit, providing the exercise is within the students' linguistic range. Otherwise frustration can ensue!).

Questions and activities

1 Dictation is mentioned on page 104. Discuss how, and when, you would give a dictation.

2 We personalise writing tasks to make them more interesting, and relevant, to the students. What do you think of the writing task on page 97? Do you think your students would find this interesting? If it appeared in your textbook, how would you amend it, in order to make it more relevant?

3 On page 101 you will find the suggestion that teachers might draw up a list of situations in which students might wish to write in English. Draw up a list for your students.

4 Look at example 6 on page 102. Devise a similar exercise based on any local tourist information you can get hold of.

5 Discuss ways in which you could find pen friends for your students.

6 Example 9 on page 106 shows how interesting writing exercises can be devised based on textbooks that may lack them. Look at the textbook you are using at the moment, and see if you can spot similar opportunities for interesting functional, personal or imaginative writing work. How would you handle it in class?

References

The examples from textbooks in this chapter have been taken from the following books:

1 *Starting English* by Joanna Gray, p 24 (Cassell EFL 1981)
2 *Discoveries 1* by Brian Abbs and Ingrid Freebairn, p 11 (Longman 1986)
3 *New Generation 1* by C Granger and D Beaumont, p 41 (Heinemann 1986)
4 *New Dimensions 1* by J Lonergan and K Gordon, p 37 (Macmillan 1986)
5 *Opening Strategies* by Brian Abbs and Ingrid Freebairn, p 34 (Longman 1982)
6 *Streamline English – Departures* by Bernard Hartley and Peter Viney, Unit 30 (Oxford University Press 1978)

# Writing skills at intermediate and advanced levels

In the last chapter we listed two main objectives:

- to enable the students to consolidate their knowledge of the language;
- to enable the students to respond appropriately in writing in those situations that require it.

These objectives are still valid at more advanced levels, but the emphasis gradually changes from the first to the second.

The first objective still remains valid, of course. At this level, there is still a need for writing activities that help to consolidate language learning. These activities may not all be really purposeful in any real-life sense. However, they can and should be personalised: this means that the teacher should make sure that they are closely related to the personal needs and interests of the students.

The teacher's decisions

As our students make progress in using the language, we need to aim at more demanding kinds of writing exercises. The question is: how demanding? We have several decisions to make:

- We have to decide if the exercises in the textbook are suitable in subject matter and level of difficulty for our students.
- If they are not, a new exercise may have to be devised, based either on the book, or on some other source. Of course, it will have to be linked in with the book in any way possible.

110

- If the exercises are suitable, we have to decide if the approach in the textbook is suitable. For example:

– does the textbook give too much help to the students? If so, then the students may find it boring and frustrating;
– does the textbook give too little help to the students? If so, they will quickly get into difficulties. They will make all kinds of mistakes. The teacher will have a headache, marking, and the students will have headaches once their work is marked!

The problems posed here have to be solved by the teacher: the textbook is not written for a particular class – and every class is different. Somehow the textbook has got to be adapted as necessary to the specific needs of a particular class in a particular situation. This is where the teacher's role is crucial.

Example 1

Let us suppose we have a class of younger students. The unit in the textbook focusses on describing events that took place in the past, using the simple past tense. Let us suppose that the unit contains only very boring writing exercises. In this situation, we should consider what the students are interested in, and find an exercise to suit them. In this example, the teacher decides to go outside the textbook and use a comic strip from a newspaper[1] (see page 111).

There are two possible approaches. In both cases, the students end up by completing the story in the box below:

1 If the comic strip has words printed in English, it can be used for reading before doing the writing exercise below.
2 If the comic strip is printed in a foreign language, then the students can be invited, again in pairs, to work out what they say in English. Use whitener to erase the words, and the students become advertising copy-writers.

> Sam and the thieves
> Sam was riding along the road on his motorcycle when he . . . a woman screaming for help. He . . . two men attacking her. They . . . her to the ground and . . . her handbag. Then they . . . away down a narrow path. It . . . too narrow for a police car, but it . . . too narrow for Sam's motorcycle. He . . . after the thieves and . . . them. The policemen . . . along soon afterwards. The policemen . . . Sam very much, but Sam . . .:
> '. . . . .!'

Often however, there is no need to go outside the textbook for ideas. As we saw in the example of the letter to an 'Agony Aunt' in the last chapter, the textbook often contains unexpected opportunities for teaching writing more creatively.

Example 2

Do you remember the newspaper story about the woman who dressed up as a man in order to get a job? (See page 62.) This is a good example of a reading passage that can stimulate both speechwork, and communicative writing practice.

A good way to follow up the reading exercise would be with a half-dialogue or role-play activity. For example, the students could act out a dialogue in which the sacked employee, Miss Mwania, tries to persuade her employer to take her back. There are several ways this could be done in class:

- The teacher gives the students a 'framework' of half-completed sentences. They decide how to complete them in pairs. Then different pairs come and act out the dialogue.
- The teacher gives the students one speaker's half of the dialogue. The students work out the other half in pairs – and then perform it as before.
- The students improvise the dialogue, the teacher putting up useful words and phrases as they do so. The students then write the dialogue.

Example 3

Maybe we don't want them to write a dialogue however, maybe we want them to write a story. In this case, we could give our students a different writing exercise, as follows:

Assignment

The story of Miss Mwania is incomplete. Imagine you are a newspaper reporter. Make up your own headline – and then write a report saying what happened in the end. If you wish, use this framework:

(HEADLINE)

The story of Miss Mwania, the girl from Kakamega who got a job after dressing up as a man, has had a happy/unhappy ending. Her employer, Mr X of Notco, has decided to . . .

Questioned by our reporters, Miss Mwania said: 'I am deeply upset/absolutely delighted . . .'

What of her plans for the future?

Obviously, in such exercises, it is for the teacher to decide just how much help the students need to write a satisfactory answer. In this assignment, they are given a lead-in sentence to get them going, but the students are still given considerable choice in what they write. It is up to them to decide how the story ended – happily, or unhappily. This exercise is thus one stage ahead of the *Suzuki* exercise: the students are encouraged to develop their own story lines, yet they are still given enough assistance to ensure that they do a reasonable job.

Of course, this is not an authentic piece of writing: but it is purposeful in an imaginative sense, and the students would enjoy doing it. Students who have done this exercise have come up with all kinds of ending: someone made up a story about how the Notco boss fell in love with Miss Mwania, and how they got married and lived happily ever after. In another version, the heroine ends up in jail. A third described how Miss Mwania went into business, and ended up buying Notco, and sacking her former boss!

What are the lessons of example 3?

- Writing assignments should be closely linked with other activities in the classroom.
- Assignments must be interesting and relevant to the students.
- It is our job to decide how much assistance to give to the students – enough to help them to write a good answer, but not so much that they are allowed no room for their own ideas.

Different kinds of pairwork

So far in these two chapters on writing, we have emphasised the value of preparatory work in pairs. 'Two heads are better than one' has been the slogan. In example 2 – writing the dialogue – it would be a good idea if the students worked in pairs: it could be a difficult exercise, and preparing a dialogue in pairs is obviously going to produce better performances.

But what about example 3? Would the students want to write this story in pairs? Or would they prefer to think up their own stories? With more open-ended and imaginative writing tasks such as this, there is a lot to be said for encouraging the students to come up with their own individual answers first. Let them use their own imagination. In this case, it is probably enough to set them going by having a brief class discussion first. They can then write a rough draft of their story individually. After this is the time to go into pairs. They can read through each other's work, pointing out errors and thus practise critical reading skills.

Writing purposes

As our students progress, they will grow increasingly more sophisticated in their use of language and, in particular, about adapting the way they write for different purposes. Thus a letter to a bank manager requesting a loan, a personal letter to a friend, an essay about a novel, and a speech for a debate will obviously not all be written in the same way.

It is quite common for a textbook to include a writing exercise where there is no apparent purpose. When this happens, the teacher can help. Before setting any writing task, it is a good idea to try to create a *context* for it. This means that the teacher suggests a plausible situation in which the students might be asked to write so that they have some idea at least of whom they are writing for, and what kind of task they are required to do.

Look again at example 3. Notice what a difference it makes if you indicate to the students what kind of text they have to write – and who their readers are. What could be a tiresome classroom exercise is turned into an interesting exercise in written communication.

Example 4

Many textbooks also fail to teach students to adapt their style according to their audience. On the next page you can see an example of the kind of exercise that might be suitable.[2] The students have to 'unmix' two letters – one to an uncle, and one to a close friend. As you can see, one letter is very informal – the other is also informal, but respectful too. Making stylistic judgements of this kind is one of the most difficult things students need to learn: so this exercise, if it seems easy, is still appropriate even for relatively advanced students. Like so many of these exercises, this one might be done by the students orally in pairs before writing.

> This is one way of helping students to write in different ways to different people. Would this exercise be suitable for your students? If not, why not make up a similar one that *is* suitable?

| Dear | Uncle Wale
Jumi | | |

| Thank you very much
Thanks a lot | for your letter | Terribly sorry
I was terribly sorry |
| to hear | about your accident
that you have been ill | I do hope that it is not as
it sounds very nasty, but |
| serious as it sounds
knowing you you'll soon bounce back! | My father
Tunde | is writing |
| separately, but in the meantime | for goodness sake do drop us a
please let us know | |
| line | if | there is anything we can do to assist
you need anything | Here's to a very
We are all praying |
| speedy recovery!
for your quick recovery | Sorry
I am very sorry indeed | that | I shall not be
you won't be |
| able to see you
able to make it- | but | I daresay we shall survive
Of course your health must come first |
| Naturally I am very disappointed, but parties always go with
It's a great pity, though- | I am sure we can meet some | |
| a swing when you're around!
other time. | Please | give my greetings to
remember me to the family |
| everyone. | Look forward to dropping in to see you soon.
We look forward to visiting you soon when you are better | |
| with best wishes for a speedy recovery
Get well soon. | | |

| Yours ever
Your affectionate nephew | | |

An approach to composition writing

It is a sad fact that a great many textbooks do not really *teach* composition writing – they *test* it. They test the teacher, too – often very little guidance is given to the teacher on how best to approach writing in the classroom. This applies particularly in advanced classes. Many books simply set a topic, and leave it to the teacher or students to get on with it. A possible approach that can be used under these circumstances is set out here.

An eight-stage approach to composition writing

1 Oral discussion of the topic. During this stage, the teacher might jot on the board a number of useful words, phrases, sentences or ideas. Sometimes key or 'topic' sentences – for example, the first sentence of a paragraph – might also go on the board. During this stage, the teacher should encourage the students to try to approach the topic from an unusual angle, if possible – but one which enables them to *write from experience*.

2 Individual planning. The students jot down their ideas in note form. Some do this paragraph by paragraph, others prefer to jot them down as they come to them, more or less randomly. The teacher helps out where necessary.
3 The students then write the composition, usually in rough first. Even professional writers don't get it right first time!
4 They check it through, possibly in cooperation with a fellow student, and amend it as necessary.
5 They hand it in for marking.
6 The teacher hands the work back, marked, and discusses it with the students, drawing attention to any common problems, etc.
7 Corrections. Sometimes at least, students should be given the opportunity of writing out a corrected version of their work.
8 Follow-up. Problems diagnosed during this exercise are treated in later lessons to prevent them from re-occurring.

This approach works quite well. It has the great advantage that in stage 1, the teacher and students discuss a few ideas first, before the students start to write. This oral phase is very important. The approach is also very flexible – there are several useful variations possible. For example, certain topics can be treated by the students working in pairs at different stages.

This approach is a help to some students at least, but it should be noted that many people find it difficult to plan in advance, and much prefer to make a start (or several false starts) and 'follow their pens'. It is surprising how ideas can flow into people's minds as ink flows from their pens. However, the best advice is this: our students should always try to write about things they know about: *we always write and talk best about things that are within our own experience.*

Summary

1 When the writing exercises in the textbook are not relevant to the personal needs and interests of our students, we should replace them. Often, authentic material such as newspaper reports and advertisements can be used.
2 Such materials offer many opportunities for use in different ways. The teacher has to decide how to do this, bearing in mind the need to fit in with the aims of the unit in the textbook.
3 Writing should be integrated with other activities – any of which can act as a useful preparation for writing.

4 One of the problems is for the teacher to decide the format of the exercise, so that it is at a suitable level of difficulty.
5 Discussion, either on a whole class basis, or in groups or pairs, can play an important part in the writing process.
6 At advanced levels, textbooks often fail to give sufficient help to the learners, and writing exercises test more than they train. When this is the case, the teacher should offer extra help.
7 One possibility for teaching composition is the eight-stage approach, which involves oral preparation, planning in advance, and writing a rough draft. This can be an efficient approach, but it does not always suit every student (or every subject).
8 When in doubt, students should always try to write simply and directly about their own experience.

Questions and activities

1 Are there any exercises in your textbook that suffer from any of the following deficiencies?

   – The exercise is not sufficiently related to the experience and interests of the students.
   – The exercise does not give enough assistance to the students before they start writing.
   – The exercise is not true-to-life, and is therefore lacking in any real purpose.
   How would you amend such exercises in your textbook?
2 Plan a writing lesson based on the eight-stage approach outlined on page 115. Pay particular attention to the words and sentences that you would put on the board in stage 1 of the lesson. (You may wish to depart from the suggested stages in various ways. If so, suggest reasons why you adapted the approach.)
3 'We always write best about things that are within our own experience'. Find some examples of your students' work that illustrate this point. How might you use these examples in class to improve your students' writing?

References

1 *Secondary English Project 1* by N Grant, D Olagoke and K Southern, p 14 (Longman 1975)
2 *Junior Secondary English Project Book 3* by N Grant, C Agunwa and D Olagoke, p 107 (Longman 1986)

Choosing and evaluating textbooks

Sometimes of course we have no choice: we *have* to use a book that someone else has chosen. That is fine if you think that the book is good; if you think it isn't, then, sooner or later, someone may ask you 'Well, what have you got against it? Have you got any better ideas as to what book we should use?' This chapter will help you to answer this question.

Of course, the perfect textbook does not exist; but the best book available for you and your students certainly does. Such a book should satisfy three conditions:

- It should suit the needs, interests and abilities of your students.
- It should suit *you*. (The best book in the world won't work in your classroom if you have good reasons for disliking it.)
- The textbook must meet the needs of official public teaching syllabuses or examinations.

Many teachers may say, at this point: 'That's all very well. But where I teach, it's the last condition that counts. The books I would like to use aren't allowed – we're not supposed to use them. Textbooks are accepted, or rejected, according to whether they cover the national syllabus laid down by the authorities. We don't choose them – they are chosen for us.'

Even if you are in this situation, it is still important to be able to evaluate the books you are using on some sensible, principled basis. This process of evaluation is the first step towards deciding how a book should be most profitably used in your classroom – and how it should be adapted.

Evaluation – a three-stage process

Evaluating a textbook is rather like buying a new coat. When we do this, we usually have to ask three questions:

1 Does it fit?
2 If it fits, how well does it fit – and how does it compare with others that also fit?
3 (Later!) Does it still fit? This question becomes relevant after you have had it for a time.

The three stages of evaluation, then, are as follows:

1 initial evaluation;
2 detailed evaluation;
3 in-use evaluation.

Let us look at these three stages of evaluation in more detail.

1 Initial evaluation

We often need to assess quickly whether a textbook is likely to be worth looking at more closely. We don't want to waste time! So in our initial evaluation, we want to filter out obviously unsuitable materials. However, we should try to avoid making judgements that are too hasty, particularly if the textbook appears to be rather unusual in its format. We should resist any perhaps natural tendencies to favour what seems familiar.

It is not easy to evaluate a textbook in a short time. Most of us have had the experience of publishers' representatives calling round and dazzling us with their new books. Many of these books are beautifully presented, with jazzy covers, and attractive artwork which distracts the eye, and dulls the brain. Sometimes, we are under some pressure to make a quick decision. Resist this pressure! Instead, decide if the book is worth looking at more closely.

One way of finding out whether a book is worth looking at more closely is to apply the 'CATALYST' test. A textbook should act as a catalyst in the classroom. Like the catalyst in a chemistry laboratory, it should facilitate change. For this reason, the CATALYST test is very appropriately named. The eight letters in the word CATALYST represent the eight criteria by which we can decide whether a textbook is suitable for our classroom. (One of the main criteria – cost – goes without saying!)

The eight criteria of the CATALYST test are set out on the left. The words in the mnemonic represent the key questions we should ask ourselves:

The CATALYST test

C – Communicative?
A – Aims?
T – Teachability?
A – Available Add-ons?
L – Level?
Y – Your impression?
S – Student interest?
T – Tried and tested?

- **Communicative?** Is the textbook communicative? Will the students be able to use the language to communicate as a result of using the book? Many teachers regard this as a fundamental question.
- **Aims?** Does it fit in with our aims and objectives? These may be laid down by the authorities, or devised by ourselves.
- **Teachable?** Does the course seem teachable? Does it seem reasonably easy to use, well-organised, easy to find your way around?
- **Available Add-ons?** Are there any useful 'add-ons' – additional materials such as teacher's books, tapes, workbooks, etc? If so, are they available?
- **Level?** Does the level seem about right?
- **Your impression?** What is your overall impression of the course?
- **Student interest?** Are your students likely to find the book interesting?
- **Tried and tested?** Has the course been tried and tested in real classrooms? Where? By whom? What were the results? How do you know?

It is an unfortunate fact that many teachers, for a variety of reasons, only have the opportunity for the most cursory examination of materials before they have to reach a decision as to whether to use them. If you are placed in this position, you should at least apply the CATALYST test. CATALYST's questions are the very minimum one should ask when looking at materials for the first time.

However, the best advice is this:

- Don't make any instant decisions. Obtain specimen copies of new materials, preferably from at least two different publishers, and allow time to evaluate them properly (see the section on detailed evaluation on the next page).
- Make sure that any decision reached is a joint one – consult with your colleagues. It is very important that any decision on such an important matter is only taken after the fullest discussions with your colleagues. If there are other people available whose opinions you respect – an inspector or adviser in the Ministry of Education, teachers from other schools or colleges, and so on – ask them for their views, too.

2 Detailed evaluation

Once we have applied the CATALYST test, and decided that a textbook will do, we then have to decide how well it will do, and whether it is more, or less, suitable than other textbooks that are available. Of course, it would be ideal to try the course out. This is what many language schools do. After piloting a new course for a term or so, they then decide whether to adopt it or not.

However, piloting new materials in this way is seldom possible in public education systems. Many teachers have to rely on their own judgement in choosing new materials. In doing so, a questionnaire can be of great assistance. The rest of this unit consists mainly of a three-part questionnaire designed to help you to decide how far a coursebook meets the three conditions mentioned at the beginning of this chapter:

- does the course suit your students?
- does it suit the teacher?
- does it suit the syllabus?

Apply this three-part questionnaire to one of your textbooks *now*. If possible, apply it to two different textbooks. Discuss your findings with your colleagues.

This questionnaire can be applied to a single textbook. However, it would be more revealing to apply it to at least two, for comparison. You will find this questionnaire on pages 122, 124 and 126 of this book.

3 In-use evaluation

Once you have adopted a textbook, it is of course necessary to re-evaluate it constantly. No questionnaire, however elaborate, can give a conclusive answer to the final test: does it work in the classroom? This evaluation process should be continuous, even in situations where you do not plan, for financial or other reasons, to replace the textbook for some time. For it is only by constant evaluation that one can ensure that the teacher is the master, and not the slave, of the textbook!

You may measure how good a book is by using the questionnaire in this chapter, if you like. However, you will probably wish to modify this questionnaire in various ways, to make sure that it reflects your own particular teaching situation more closely. However you decide to monitor a book's progress in the classroom, remember to arrange regular meetings between you and your colleagues to discuss textbooks and other matters of common interest.

Choosing a textbook: questionnaire (part 1)

Does the book suit your students?

1 Is it attractive? Given the average age of your students, would they enjoy using it?	YES	PARTLY	NO
2 Is it culturally acceptable?	YES	PARTLY	NO
3 Does it reflect what you know about your students' needs and interests?	YES	PARTLY	NO
4 Is it about the right level of difficulty?	YES	PARTLY	NO
5 Is it about the right length?	YES	PARTLY	NO
6 Are the course's physical characteristics appropriate? (e.g. is it durable?)	YES	PARTLY	NO
7 Are there enough authentic materials, so that the students can see that the book is relevant to real life?	YES	PARTLY	NO
8 Does it achieve an acceptable balance between *knowledge about* the language, and *practice in using* the language?	YES	PARTLY	NO
9 Does it achieve an acceptable balance between the relevant language skills, and integrate them so that work in one skill area helps the others?	YES	PARTLY	NO
10 Does the book contain enough communicative activities to enable the students to use the language independently?	YES	PARTLY	NO

Score: 2 points for every YES answer.
1 point for every PARTLY answer.
0 for every NO answer.

Notes on part 1 of the questionnaire

Q1
–3
Elementary questions, of course. Yet it is amazing how often they are not given proper consideration. For example, I have seen ten-year olds using textbooks designed for adults. Do we really want school children to learn, 'American Express? That will do nicely!'?

Q4 To answer this, we should look not just at different parts of the book in isolation, but at the book's gradient: is the speed at which new items of language are introduced too fast (or too slow) for the students?

Q5 It can be very discouraging for learners to be stuck with a coursebook for too long. Psychologically, the ideal is to finish a book by the end of a term or year. This can give both students and teachers a sense of achievement.

Q6 An important consideration, particularly in schools where it is expected that books will be handed on. However, durability is not the only factor. One course failed because the books would not fit into the children's school bags!

Q7 'Authentic materials' means anything that is not primarily designed for textbook use. Examples of authentic reading materials might include advertisements, letters, postcards, newspaper reports, football or theatre programmes, appropriate literature, etc.

Q8/9 Only you know your students well enough to know what the balance should be. 'Knowledge about the language' includes at least *some* basic 'rules of thumb' about its grammar.

Q10 Very important: your students will appreciate a book that will enable them to communicate in real life. (See page 14 for some examples of communicative activities.)

Choosing a textbook: questionnaire (part 2)

Does the book suit the teacher?

1 Is your overall impression of the contents and layout of the course favourable?	YES	PARTLY	NO
2 Is there a good, clear teacher's guide with answers and help on methods and additional activities?	YES	PARTLY	NO
3 Can one use the book in the classroom without constantly having to turn to the teacher's guide?	YES	PARTLY	NO
4 Are the recommended methods and approaches suitable for you, your students and your classroom?	YES	PARTLY	NO
5 Are the approaches easily adaptable if necessary?	YES	PARTLY	NO
6 Does using the course require little or no time-consuming preparation?	YES	PARTLY	NO
7 Are useful ancillary materials such as tapes, workbooks, and visuals provided?	YES	PARTLY	NO
8 Is there sufficient provision made for tests and revision?	YES	PARTLY	NO
9 Does the book use a 'spiral' approach, so that items are regularly revised and used again in different contexts?	YES	PARTLY	NO
10 Is the course appropriate for, and liked by, colleagues?	YES	PARTLY	NO

Score: 2 points for every YES answer.
1 point for every PARTLY answer.
0 for every NO answer.

Notes on part 2 of the questionnaire

Q1   The key word here is 'overall'. There will always be certain minor things about the textbook – either what it contains, or the way it is designed on the page – that you dislike.

Q2/3   Not all teachers think this is important – personally, I do. Additional ideas at least are always welcome. But the textbook should not be so complicated that constant reference to a teacher's manual is necessary.

Q4/5   These questions are also important: many attractive courses seem designed especially for small classes, and the methods suggested don't work very well in big classes unless they can be modified.

Q6/7   No one expects to be able to step into a classroom without any preparation. However, as teachers we are generally short of time, and we therefore appreciate materials that do not place unnecessary burdens on us.

Q8   This area is often neglected in textbooks. Good textbooks contain diagnostic tests that help teachers to find out individual students' problem areas, as well as progress tests to give some idea of how well they are progressing.

Q9   It is very important that a language function and/or a grammatical form (such as a verb tense used in a particular way) should reappear several times after being introduced, for revision, practice, and extension.

Q10   It is a very good idea if all teachers take part in the process of selection. If teachers feel that books are just imposed on them without consideration of their views, they may resent them. An exchange of views about textbooks, and methods, is very healthy.

Choosing a textbook: questionnaire (part 3)

Does the textbook suit the syllabus and examination?

1 Has the book been recommended or approved by the authorities?	YES	PARTLY	NO
2 Does the book follow the official syllabus in a creative manner?	YES	PARTLY	NO
3 Is the course well-graded, so that it gives well-structured and systematic coverage of the language?	YES	PARTLY	NO
4 If it does more than the syllabus requires, is the result an improvement?	YES	PARTLY	NO
5 Are the activities, contents and methods used in the course well-planned and executed?	YES	PARTLY	NO
6 Has it been prepared specifically for the target examination?	YES	PARTLY	NO
7 Do the course's methods help the students prepare for the exam?	YES	PARTLY	NO
8 Is there a good balance between what the examination requires, and what the students need?	YES	PARTLY	NO
9 Is there enough examination practice?	YES	PARTLY	NO
10 Does the course contain useful hints on examination technique?	YES	PARTLY	NO

Score: 2 points for every YES answer.
1 point for every PARTLY answer.
0 for every NO answer.

Notes on part 3 of the questionnaire

Q1/2   Note that in some countries you can get into trouble if you use books that have not been recommended.

Q3   'From the simple to the complex, from the known to the unknown' are two tried and tested principles. In general, what the students learn earlier in the course should help them to learn what comes later more easily.

Q4   Most syllabuses are intended to be useful guides rather than infallible directives. A book which follows the spirit of a syllabus as well as the letter can usually improve on it in all kinds of ways.

Q5   A good textbook should not of course consist merely of
–8   'examination format' exercises endlessly rehearsing examination questions. Obviously the textbook should be relevant to the examination. However, it should also be relevant to the students' communicative needs. If the examination does not reflect these needs, the teacher's job is to find an acceptable middle way.

Q9   No one wants the textbook to be merely 'an exam crammer'. But it is our duty to our students to ensure that when they finally go into the examination, there will be no nasty surprises – unfamiliar question formats, and the like.

Q10   We all know that examination results are at least partly determined by examination technique.

NOTE

Part 3 of this questionnaire may not apply to you for either of the following reasons:

1 You do not have an official syllabus. In this case, the book should be compared with the syllabus you use. But remember, this may result in amending the syllabus, rather than rejecting the textbook.

2 Your students may not be entering for an examination. In this case, questions 6–10 are not applicable.

Questions and activities

1 These questionnnaires are unlikely to be perfect for every teaching situation. Are there any questions you would like to amend or replace in some way? Perhaps you think there should be a question about the cost of a course, for instance! If so, in which part would it go – 1, 2 or 3? Give reasons for any changes you think should be made.

2 Apply these questionnaires to the coursebooks that you are using. Discuss the results. How far do you agree with other people's results? If there are differences of opinion, how do you account for them?

3 You will notice that there is some overlap between some of the questions, and that a question in one part of the questionnaire could also be asked in a different part. Can you find some examples?

4 Which of these three questionnaires is the most important? Is it possible to single one out as being the most crucial – or are they all equally important?

5 Is there anything that these questionnaires reveal about a course that the CATALYST tests do not?

6 Another way of designing this kind of questionnaire is by listing a series of statements, and measuring the truth of each against a five-point scale, as in this example for questionnnaire 1.

1 The book is suitable for my students' age group. 4 3 2 1 0

With this method, 4 means 'Ideal', 3 means 'Very suitable', 2 means 'Suitable', 1 means 'Not very suitable', and 0 means 'Unsuitable'. Would you prefer this type of questionnaire?

The questionnnaires in this chapter are designed for main coursebooks. Design similar questionnaires for either supplementary textbooks or supplementary readers. Try out the questionnaires. You may well have to amend them as a result of trying them out!